SEO Made Easy

Training Guide

Quickstart Guide to Skyrocket Your Offline and Online Business with Search Engines

<u>Disclaimer:</u>

This work may not be copied, sold, used as content in any manner or your name put on it until you buy sufficient rights to sell it or distribute it as your own from us and the authorized reseller/distributer.

Every effort has been made to be accurate in this publication. The publisher does not assume any responsibility for errors, omissions or contrary interpretation. We do our best to provide the best information on the subject, but just reading it does not guarantee success. You will need to apply every step of the process in order to get the results you are looking for.

This publication is not intended for use as a source of any legal, medical or accounting advice. The information contained in this guide may be subject to laws in the United States and other jurisdictions. We suggest carefully reading the necessary terms of the services/products used before applying it to any activity which is, or may be, regulated. We do not assume any responsibility for what you choose to do with this information. Use your own judgment.

Any perceived slight of specific people or organizations, and any resemblance to characters living, dead or otherwise, real or fictitious, is purely unintentional.

Some examples of past results are used in this publication; they are intended to be for example purposes only and do not guarantee you will get the same results. Your results may differ from ours. Your results from the use of this information will depend on you, your skills and effort, and other different unpredictable factors.

It is important for you to clearly understand that all marketing activities carry the possibility of loss of investment for testing purposes. Use this information wisely and at your own risk.

Table of Content

Introduction:

Welcome to the latest and most effective **SEO Training Guide** designed to guide you through the process of easily and effectively positioning your offline or online business at the top of any Search Engine on the web. We are excited to have you here and we know this will be very helpful for you.

This complete and high-quality training guide will surely help you to learn everything there is to know in order to easily and effectively **position your online or offline business on the first Page of the Search Engines in the shortest time possible,** as well as how to leverage this amazing and extremely powerful source of high quality traffic to generate great profits online.

You will be able to **quickly and safely grow a huge army of potential clients or customers 100% targeted to your business**. Search Engines have the amazing ability to send highly relevant traffic to any website that is positioned on their top page, and this is just an amazing thing that can bring you great results.

You will be able to **rank any amount of pages of your website straight to the top** and get a great deal of high quality and unique search engine traffic to each one of them. You will able to know the exact same **Search Engine Top Ranking Proven Formula** we use, which is responsible for ranking any brand new webpage to the top of the Search Engines with the safest and easiest techniques ever.

Google is a fantastic platform, with which you can reach all of your business plans, but we will also focus on all search engines. If you win the Google battle then you will be at the top of all the search engines at the same time.

This high-quality training guide contains everything you need to know about ranking in the top of the search engines to help you achieve your goals.

10 Simple Steps are more than enough

10 very easy to follow steps are more than enough for you to get the most out of the search engines.

- You don't have to worry about wasting your time.
- You don't have to worry about ineffective strategies.
- You don't have to worry about wasting your money on other training.

The only thing you have to be worry about is reading every single word of this guide and applying it.

Millions of dollars have been invested on every search engine since they started in order to give outstanding benefits to you and your business. This excellent course will take you by the hand and show you step-by-step, topic by topic and tool by tool what you really need to know in order to position your business at the top the easiest way possible, using the most effective tools and in the shortest time ever.

Chapter I: What is SEO?

Search Engine Optimization (SEO): consists of a set of optimization techniques applied to a website or webpage to position it at the top of the search engines results based on a keyword or set of keywords on which that website or webpage has been optimized for.

For easy understanding the process works like this:

A lady uses a search engine to search for something she is interested in finding information about. In this case we will use Google.com as our search engine example. All search engines work similar, like Yahoo and Bing, which are the best after Google.

After she performs her search; the first page of Google displays a set of highly relevant pages or domains right in front of her so she may get access to any one of them that might give the information she is looking for.

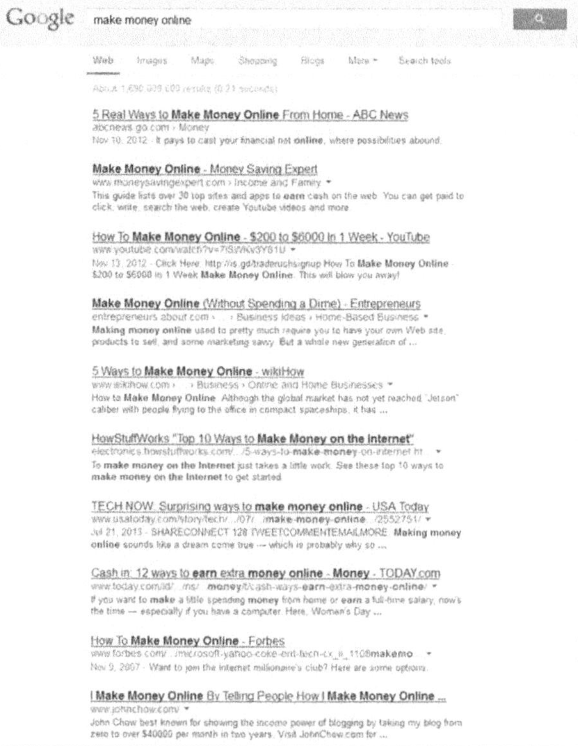

Every one of those websites have been in some degree optimized in order for the Google Search Engine Bot (Google Algorithm) to consider them exactly what the searcher is looking for and place them right there in the top page, as well as in the top positions of the first page.

Search Engine ranking is all about a battle where the best optimized webpages are picked by the search engines to be placed in the top and grab the eyes of all the searchers.

Chapter II: Why Search Engine Traffic?

Search engine traffic is known as the most high quality traffic ever. The higher the quality of the traffic you send to your webpages, the greatest the benefits you will get from it (Sales, Subscribers, etc.)

There are 2 types of Search Engine Traffic. The Paid search engine traffic and the Free search engine traffic.

The Paid search engine traffic is the practice of placing your website on the sponsored search engine section of the top page. That is something a lot more easily achieved because you buy that spot and pay to the search engine by view or by click.

The Free search engine traffic is the practice of placing your website on the natural search engine section of the top page by applying specific on page and off page optimization techniques to your webpage. This is something a little bite difficult to achieve and requires time, but is 100% free of charge from the Search Engines.

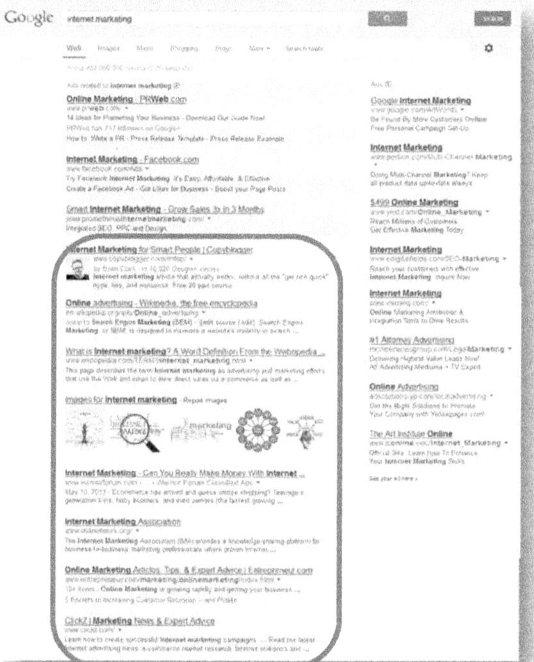

The second one is what we are going after on this high quality and step-by-step training and the difficult part of this search engine traffic approach might easily be taken down thanks to the specific techniques we will show in our training. So you don't waste your time, money and efforts.

Chapter III: Why SEO?

As stated before, Search engine traffic is the greatest traffic ever you could wish to get to your website in order to build a highly successful business over the web that may last years to come. Let me show you some crazy Eye Opening Facts about SEO that will help you to understand why SEO is something that can add unlimited value to your business over the web:

Eye Opening SEO facts:

Online visitors make frequent use of search engines to find products and content.	
	Users believe that the website links at the top of a search engine are the most credible or relevant.
Top ranking sites make more profit from increased online traffic.	
	Users have a tendency to use another search engine, rather than stay on a search engine that has insufficient results on the first page.
Less than 25% of users search the second page of search engines.	
	Over 50% of online buyers purchase products from websites found via search engines.
Over 60% of users search sites on the first page of search engines.	
	Over 80% of users use search engines to find a website.
Over 70% of users like to use the web to find out about new products.	
	70% of the links that search engine users click on are organic.

80% of users ignore the paid ads, focusing on the organic results.	
	75% of users never scroll past the first page of search results.
Search and e-mail are the top two Internet activities.	
	Companies that blog have 434% more indexed pages, and companies with more indexed pages get far more leads.
81% of businesses consider their blogs to be an important asset to their businesses.	
	A study by Outbrain shows that search is the #1 driver of traffic to content sites, beating social media by more than 300%
SEO leads have a 14.6% close rate, while outbound leads (such as direct mail or print advertising) have a 1.7% close rate.	
	79% of search engine users say they frequently click on the natural search results. In contrast, 80% of search engine users say they occasionally/rarely/never click on the sponsored search results.

When you see data like this you really have to believe that there is a lot of money to be made in here. Many people might be talking about it, but very few can really teach how to productively position your business there and make money with it at the same time.

By the end of the 10 steps outlined in our training guide, you will know everything you need to know to be able to scale your business online a lot more with the Search Engines.

Chapter IV: The 10 Steps to SEO Success

Here are the 10 vital steps you will need to follow in order to get the most out of the Search Engines for your business over the web:

Step 1: Pick a hot Product... Guarantee your Income...

Step 2: Find a massive Audience... Guarantee your Traffic...

Step 3: Assure Accessibility... Guarantee your Efforts...

Step 4: Register a Domain Name... the right one...

Step 5: Setting up your hosting... cheaply and safely...

Step 6: Website building... Setting up your SEMMM...

Step 7: Creating Content... high-quality content please...

Step 8: Affiliate Connection... click-magnet technique...

Step 9: Final tweaks... absolutely necessary...

Step 10: Link Building... the stuff that really works...

Step 1: Pick a hot product... Guarantee your Income...

At the very beginning I knew your questions would be:

- ✓ What topic is selling online?
- ✓ What should I promote?
- ✓ How much money can I make with this topic?
- ✓ Are people actually making money with this topic over the web?
- ✓ Are there great and high converting affiliate products on this topic?

And you can answer to all of them and to many more at the same time by finding a hot selling product right before you start doing anything else. A lot of people start searching for keywords or building a website in a topic they think is hot, but that's not where it all starts.

For that reason this makes it the most important step so you can make the greatest decision right before you put all your efforts into your future Search Engine money making machine.

The first thing you need to do is search the weapon you will use in order to make money online by sending high quality traffic to that offer. If you already have a product you would like to market online using the search engines, what you need to do is to spy on similar products and see their actual profit margins.

There is no need for you to search the entire Internet for a hot product to promote. You can just look into the most used affiliate networks online and spend just a few minutes to find one.

If your intention is to sell physical products you can just go to Amazon.com and take a look at the best-selling products over there. You can go to that section by <u>clicking here</u>

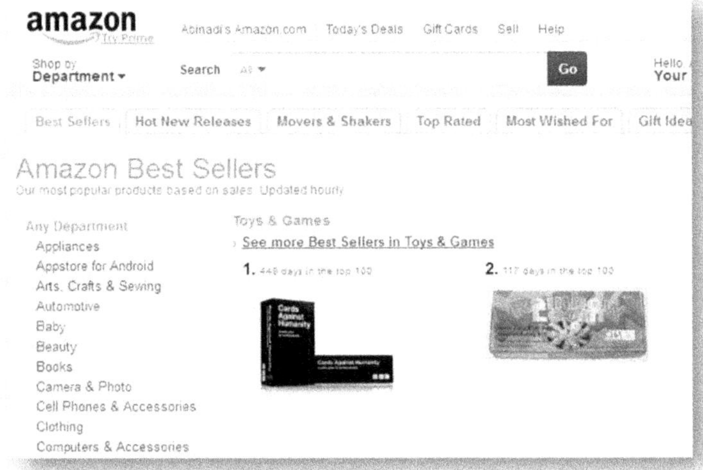

Here you have the chance to find the best selling products and pick a really hot one so you can sell it yourself or promote it, either way you know the product is hot to sell online and you will get to make money with it as well.

If you would like to go into an even more profitable marketing approach you could immerse yourself into the digital information products world, which is responsible for generating millions and millions of dollars-- all to affiliates.

You can have a look at ClickBank to find a lot of amazing digital products that are already having great selling success over the Internet. You can go there too by <u>clicking here</u>.

You will need to open a free account in order to get access to the ClickBank marketplace.

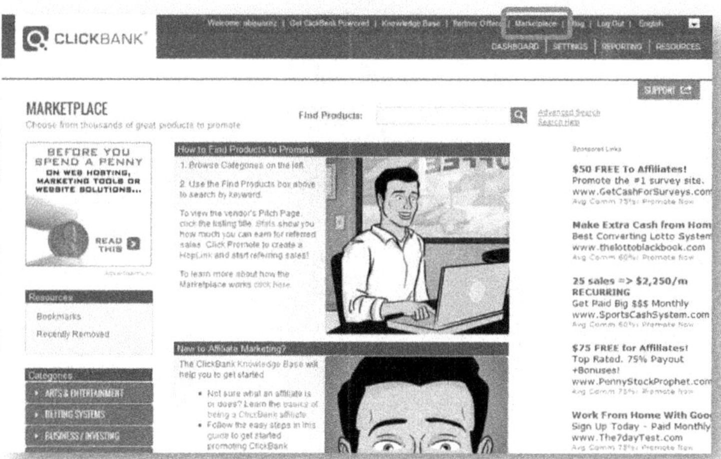

I will use the Digital Product Approach throughout the whole training so you may know how to make great money promoting ClickBank products with free search engine traffic.

Right here you can see all the categories you can chose from to find a hot selling product.

I will take a look at the Patenting & Families Category.

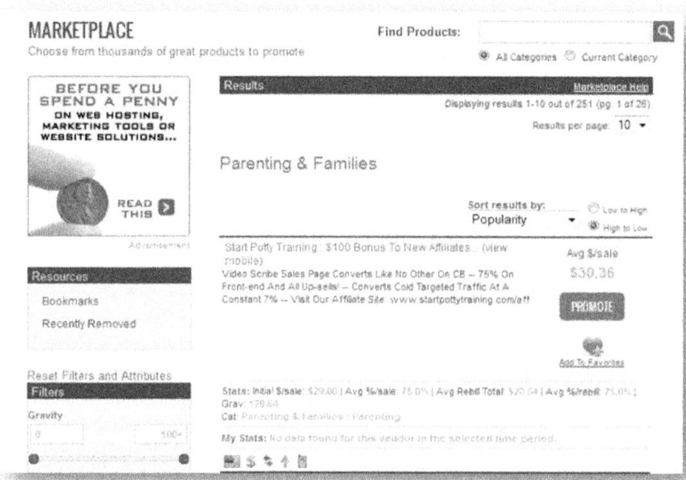

You can even sort them by different factors. I will sort it by Gravity.

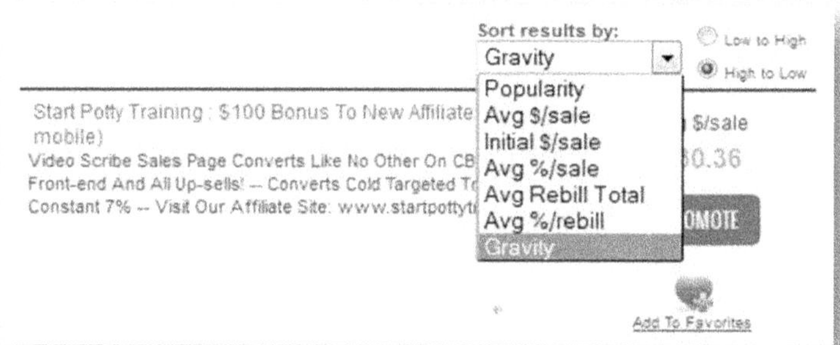

Gravity means a score given by ClickBank about the amount of affiliates that have made a sale lately promoting the product.

Let's have a look into this product right here.

As you can see, this product sells like crazy, as this is something people interested in potty training their kids will definitely be interested at having a look into to see if it fits their needs.

In this example we can say that around 120 affiliates on average have made a sale lately promoting this product. That's awesome; the product's conversion is alive.

Imagine how much money you could make by achieving just 1 sale every day promoting this product. That will be 30 sales every month, that's around $900 every single month with just one product.

The amount of sales will depend on the amount of high quality traffic you send to the offer, and that amount of traffic will depend on the keywords you chose to advertise that offer on the search engines. We will talk about that in the next step.

Something additional you can give a look about picking the perfect product to promote is by knowing how much money in total that product can give you per sale.

This dollar amount right here (Avg $/sale $30.36) will tell you how much money you can expect to get by every front sell you make as an affiliate of the product, the higher this number, the higher the commission for you.

This symbol right here will tell you if the product has up-sales. An up-sale means that after a buyer has paid for the product he/she will be redirected to a hotter offer that can deliver a lot more benefits or stuff that will make the process easier to the buyer in order to achieve what he/she is looking for to satisfy with the product, a great percentage of them will buy that up-sale.

This dollar amount right here (Avg Rebill Total: $20.54) will tell you if the product has a monthly payment subscription. This is an amazing feature where the buyer may have access to a greater quality training on the same subject, as well as having access to the latest information just for staying as a member.

These 3 highly important components will tell you the real profit potential you can get by promoting a specific product of your choice. Now you can easily say that:

- ✓ This topic is selling great online
- ✓ You finally know what to promote.
- ✓ You can easily calculate how much money you can make per sale.
- ✓ You can see how a lot of affiliates are making a killing by promoting it.
- ✓ And finally, you are assured that the product is high converting

Now you are done with Step 1. It's time to find the audience that will make you money.

Step 2: Find a massive audience... Guarantee your Traffic...

Now that we have found the weapon we will use to make money online, it's time to find a hungry audience that perfectly fits into this product. We are going to find people with needs and questions whose answers will be satisfied with the product we will offer to them. Here I mean Keyword Research.

I like to call it audience research because the keywords are the representation of real people that have a common need to be satisfied.

For this we are going to use the new Google Keyword Planner. Google itself has created an extraordinary tool that can tell us the exact needs of people. The amount of times a specific keyword is used to perform a search on Google.com will tell us the size of a particular audience.

The process goes like this: A mom from (let's say New York) needs to potty train her little boy. She goes to Google.com and searches for "how to potty train a boy."

Then that search is stored in the Google Keyword Planner data together with the searches made with the exact same keyword from other States in the United States, as well as the searches made from other countries in the whole world.

All that amount of searches made is the representation of a great amount of people interested in the exact same thing, which could be satisfied using the exact same product to all of them at the same time.

The great thing about this is that this amount of searches grows over time, which increases your audience a lot more and increases your chances to make a lot more money promoting the same exact product and even other related ones.

Let's go to the Google Keyword Planner and let's find some really great keywords (huge audience) to advertise our hot selling product.

Now go directly to the Google Keyword Planner by clicking here. You will need to have a free Google account to get access to the tool.

Once inside you will click on "Search for keyword and ad group ideas":

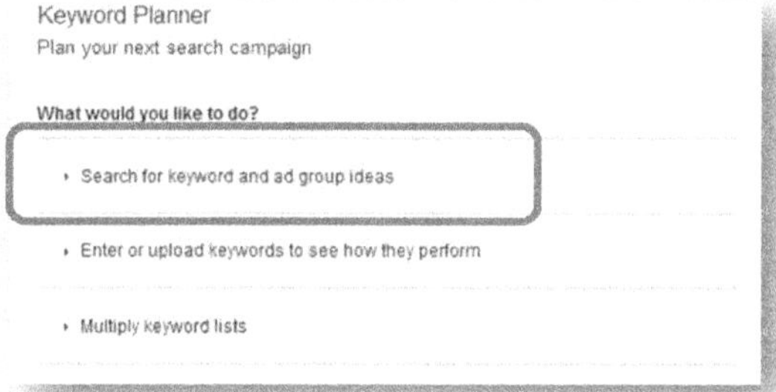

Place your Keyword; here you may search using a product name or a keyword that perfectly represents the general topic on which the product was created on.

Choose your preferences and click "get ideas."

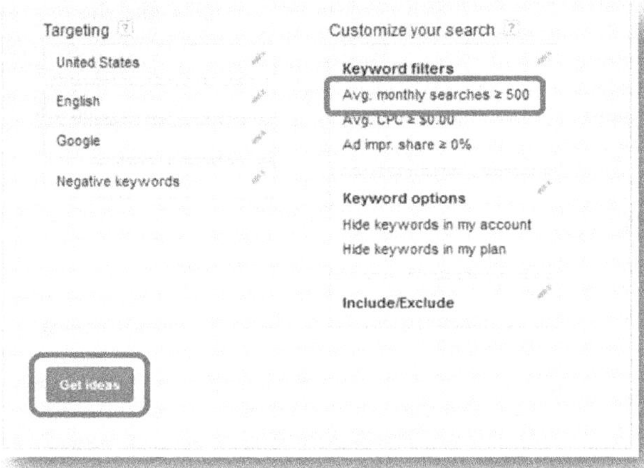

Click on "keyword ideas" and there you have a great list of keywords with a lot of monthly searches to pick from.

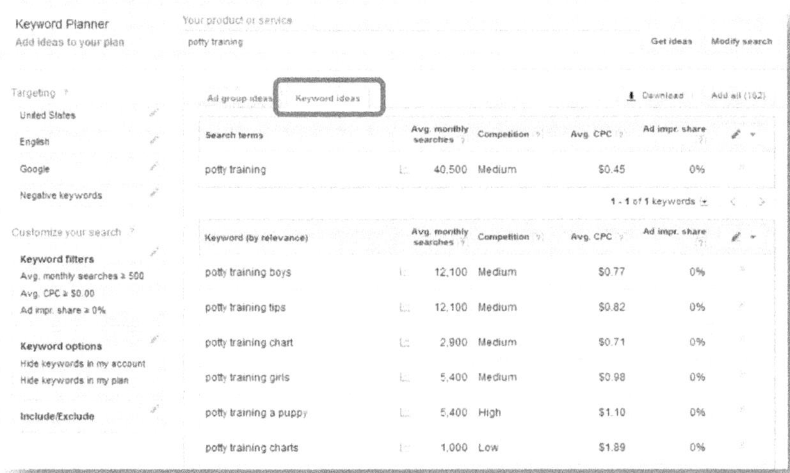

Your intention is to find as many keywords with the highest amount of searches as possible that can perfectly fit into the product you will be promoting. Every single keyword represents a specific audience and may be a completely different amount of people.

Your main goal is to get access to as many massive audiences as possible, so you may apply the 3rd step to them and see how many of them will have the chance to rank in the top of Google with a brand new mini site that you are going to create.

To be honest, the Google Keyword Planner is not that good at finding relevant keywords at the same time, because you have to run it many times with different variations so you may collect as many keywords as possible.

For that reason there is a really cool free tool called **Keyword Funnel Software** that will help you to find as many keywords as you want with a single click of a button and then you will be able to use all those keywords in the Google Keyword Planner and get a lot of massive audiences at the same time a lot faster.

This tool is completely optional; you will need to have access to Excel from the Microsoft Office set of tools in order to run it. The great thing is that the tool is available for Excel 2003, 2007, 2010 or 2013 versions. In order to download a free copy of Keyword Funnel Software click here

Now you are done with Step 2. It's time to make sure these audiences (keywords) are accessible to place brand new webpages on top of the search engines, especially on Google.com

Step 3: Assure Accessibility... Guarantee your Efforts...

It would be really sad for you to create a great site, spending a lot of time and money without doing the proper analysis to find out if you really could have any chance to rank it at the top of Google.

Now it is time to know if it's possible for us to enter into the Google Highway (Top Page); so our website and webpages might be placed in front of their unique audiences that will satisfy their needs with the product we are promoting.

Here, you see the list of Massive Audiences or Keywords that we have discovered with the Google keyword Planner. Only for this example I have taken note of 11 keywords that have a lot of searches; 11 different audiences that may make us a lot of money once they see the great product we are promoting.

Audiences (Keywords)	Searches
potty training boys	12.100
potty training tips	12.100
how to potty train a boy	8.100
how to potty train a girl	5.400
potty training girls	5.400
3 day potty training	4.400
potty chair	2.400
potty training in 3 days	1.600
toilet training in less than a day	590
potty chairs for boys	590

You will need to make sure that all audiences (keywords) are relevant to the product, this is extremely important because you might be wasting your efforts analyzing the wrong audience, like "potty training for puppies" for this example.

What we are going to do right now is to analyze every one of the top 10 pages of Google for every one of these keywords and see what exactly those competitors are doing to get ranked at the top. We will spy them and see if we can do it better than they do.

 Remember, Google is a coded machine, if you try to mimic and do a better job than the sites that are ranking at the top for a particular keyword; is definitely possible you can outrank them. The word Ranking means that the best performer will be always on top.

For that reason there is a set of components we will need to give a look into in order to know how weak a competitor in the top of Google is and then determine how accessible the audience is to place our new websites there. Those 4 components are:

1. **Domain Authority**
2. **Page Authority**
3. **External Backlinks**
4. **YouTube Presence**

Before I give you more details on these components, let's pick a keyword among the ones we have found and let's identify our top 10 most important competitors which we are going to face in this search engine battle.

I will use "potty training boys" for this example. As you can see below, here we have the top 10 competitors ranking in Google.com with this particular term:

potty training boys

Web   Images   Maps   Shopping   Videos   More ▾   Search tools

About 7,240,000 results (0.21 seconds)

Ad related to potty training boys ⓘ

Busy Moms Potty Training - ThePottyBootCamp.com
www.thepottybootcamp.com/ ▾
Easy to follow, simple, and it works. No diapers by next week.
Success Stories - Sneak Peek - Order Now/ Preview - Our Blog

Successful potty training for boys | BabyCenter
www.babycenter.com › Toddler › Potty Training › Potty Training Details ▾
The key to potty training success is starting only when your son is truly able to do
so

How to Potty Train in a Week - Potty Training Tips for Boys & Girls ...
www.parenting.com/gallery/how-to-potty-train ▾
Trust me, potty training doesn't have to be hard or stressful. Even as a first-time
single mom with no dad in the house to help out, I managed to potty train my son ...
How to Potty Train in a Week - Best Potty Training Products

Potty Training Boys In 3 Days?
pottytrainingboys.org/ ▾
Jun 19, 2013 - Potty Training Boys Tips, Techniques, When And How To Start,
Problems You Might Encounter, Recommended Books, Free Videos, And More.

Potty Training Boys made Easy - YouTube

www.youtube.com/watch?v=tscEmPltCol
May 30, 2013 - Uploaded by Tech channel
Potty Training Boys in 3 Days How to Guide: http://bit.ly/potty-
training-boys Is your child ready for Potty ...

Potty Training Boys - YouTube

www.youtube.com/watch?v=KrRJn5JINSs
Oct 4, 2010 - Uploaded by RNK Innovations
How to potty train boys using the Potty Training in One Day
method and Potty Scotty products.

How to Potty Train A Boy - Scary Mommy
www.scarymommy.com/how-to-potty-train-a-boy/ ▾
parenting BY dummies is a humor, lifestyle blog written by the best mom in the
world. In her free time she enjoys losing weight easily, looking like a soap star the ...

Potty Training Tips for Boys - Parents
www.parents.com › ... › Potty Training › Potty Training Tips ▾
Potty training boys can be tough! To the rescue: Jen Singer, author of the Stop
Second-Guessing Yourself guides to parenting and Pull-Ups Potty Training ...

Potty training for boys - BabyCentre
www.babycentre.co.uk/a548355/potty-training-for-boys ▾
A complete guide to potty training your son. - BabyCentre.

Easy Ways to Potty Train Boys - Moms - Popsugar
moms.popsugar.com/Easy-Ways-Potty-Train-Boys-27330399 ▾
Mar 23, 2013 - Although many potty-training tips apply to boys and girls alike, potty
training boys does pose some unique challenges. Whether you're ...

Advice for potty training a reluctant boy - Washington Post
articles.washingtonpost.com › Collections › Twins
Jun 27, 2012 - Q: For six years I've been the nanny for three active little boys: a
6-year-old who is usually at school, and his 3-year-old twin brothers, whom I ...

This number  represents the number of competitors we would need to face with this term, but we don't need to analyze all of them, we just need to analyze and spy on the top 10 because they are the best 10 out all these millions of competitors.

In a race you wouldn't need to be worry about all of the competitors that will be competing with you, you just need to be worry about the top ones. If you do a better job than they do, then you will be the best of all then.

Now that we know who are our real competitors let's see how good they are to be able to rank at the top of Google. Let's see what Google is looking at on them that has caused them to decide to place them at the Top.

1. **Presence of Authority Domains:** for Authority Domains we mean domain names that have a really powerful presence on Google for a long time. Those Domains might be Amazon.com, Ebay.com, apple.com, Walmart.com, etc. If you see that a lot of authority domains are in the top of Google that is not a good sign, because they will be really difficult to outrank.

There is a really great way to identify the authority of a domain by using the free Open Site Explorer tool provided by Moz.com

What is Moz?

Moz is a well-established company from Seattle founded back in 2004. Their principal focus is "Online Data analysis," and they are extremely good at it.

They have recently launched what is called Moz Analysis: Extremely powerful marketing analytics software specially designed to analyze websites as deeply as possible (Search, Social, Links, Content and brand) to determine how well they perform over the web.

Moz.com has created an outstanding and powerful weapon called Open Site Explorer. With this incredible tool -that none of the Keyword Tool Creators online want you to know about- we are able to get data from Moz.com completely for free.

Open Site Explorer is powered by the Mozscape index.

87 Billion URLs | 164 Million Root Domains | 779 Billion Links

2.30%	of all links found were nofollowed
16.56%	of all pages now employ a rel=canonical tag
70	links on the average page
10.0	external links on average

38 days of data, last updated September 4, 2013, next index update: October 2, 2013

303 Million Just-Discovered Links beta

30 days of data, updated every hour

With the Open Site Explorer tool; Moz puts their powerful web crawler and index of over 85 Billion URLs in the palm of our hands. It is data already crawled that we may have access to whenever we want to perform our analyses.

The feature that I want to show you now is called **Domain Authority**, and according to Moz.com Domain Authority represents Moz's best prediction for how a website will perform in search engine rankings.

Moz calculates this metric by combining all of the other link metrics—linking root domains, number of total links, MozRank, MozTrust, etc.—into a single score.

Over 40 signals are included in this calculation. This means your website's Domain Authority score will often fluxuate. For this reason, it's best to use Domain Authority as a competitive metric against other sites as opposed to a historic measure of your internal SEO efforts. Domain Authority is scored on a 100-point, logarithmic scale. (Taken from Moz.com)

Let's take a look at the Domain Authority for the top Google website under the "potty training boys" audience:

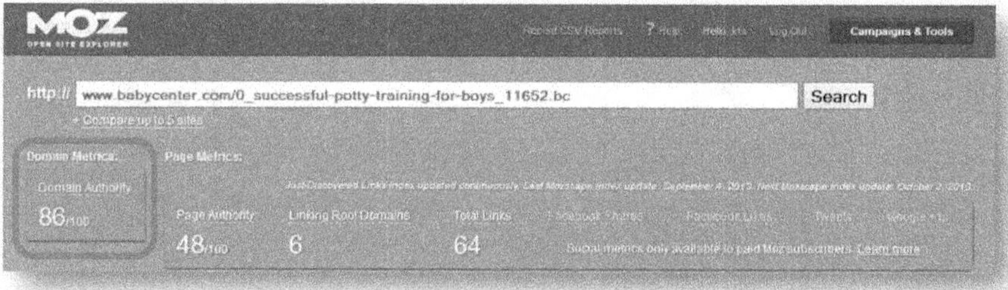

As you can see, 86 out of 100 is kind of high. This is considered an Authority Domain. I myself like to be below 50 points to consider the Domain an easier target to beat. Remember the lower the weaker and easier it is to outrank.

2. Presence of Authority Pages: now let's see what Moz has to offer about the ranking potential of a specific Page.

Page Authority is Moz's calculated metric for how well a given webpage is likely to rank in Google.com's search results. It is based off of data from the Mozscape web index and includes link counts, MozRank, MozTrust, and dozens of other factors.

It uses a machine learning model to predictively find an algorithm that best correlates with rankings across the thousands of search results that they predict against.

Whereas Page Authority measures the predictive ranking strength of a single page, Domain Authority measures the strength of entire domains or subdomains. Page Authority is scored on a 100-point, logarithmic scale as well.

(Taken from Moz.com)

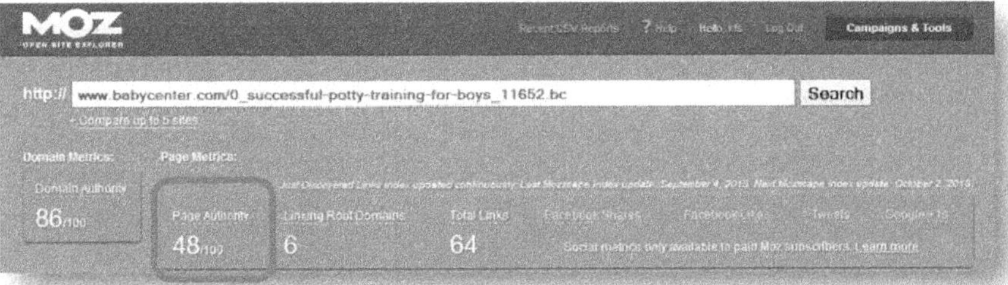

Here we see that the score is right in the middle. I also prefer to be below 50 points for page authority. Remember, the lower the weaker and easier it is to outrank.

3. External Backlinks: for a backlink (or link) we mean a hyperlink that is pointing to a specific place of a website (a page or to the domain itself). Backlinks may be internal or external. Internal backlinks are all those links pointing to different parts inside of the domain itself, like a link located in the home page liking to another one of its pages.

External Backlinks are the links that point at (target) any domain other than the domain the link exists on (source).

If another website links to you, this is considered an external link to your site. Similarly, if you link out to another website, this is also considered an external link.

Experienced SEOs believe that external links are the most important source of ranking power. This is because external links pass "link juice" (ranking power) differently than internal links because the search engines consider them as third-party votes. (Taken from Moz.com)

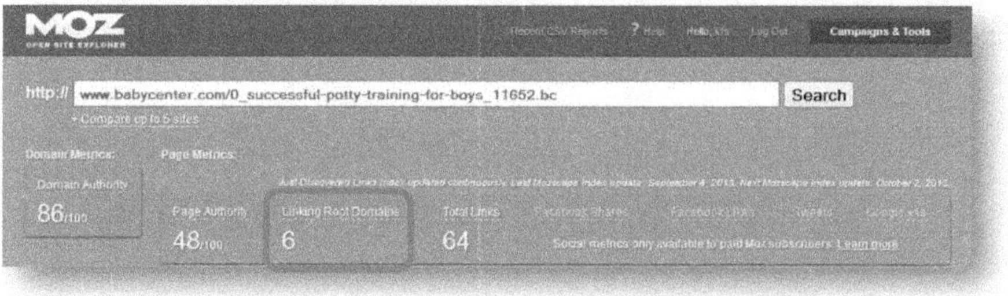

Here we may also see that only 6 external links (or unique external domains) are pointing to this URL. This is very low and it can be considered as a really easy to beat page. I myself like to find a number below 50 as well. Remember the lower the weaker and easier it is to outrank.

4. YouTube Presence: the presence of YouTube videos at the top are a great indicator of an easy to rank keyword. YouTube Videos are really easy to rank too. In that way you may rank a YouTube video and use the description box to place a link to the page you want to rank at the top of Google at the same time. The higher the number of spots you take at the top of Google will give you a lot more chances to cover the whole audience.

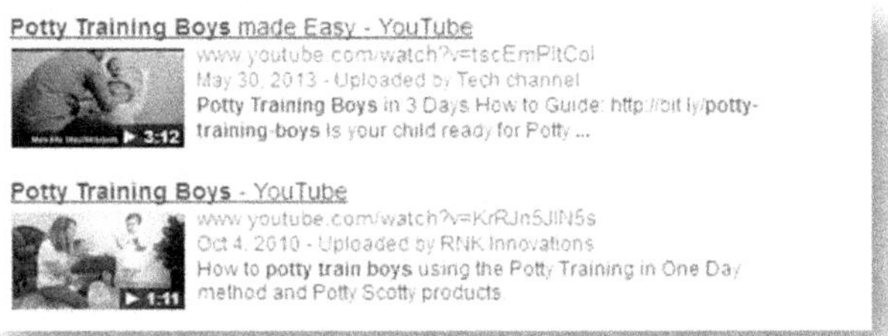

There are 2 YouTube videos right there at the top. And they seem very easy to outrank as well with your own YouTube video.

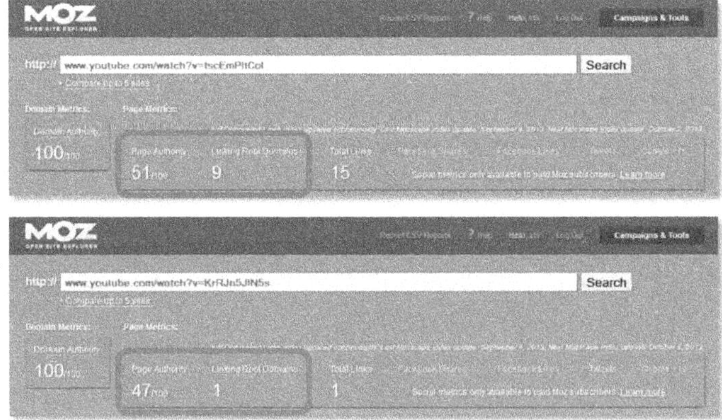

Don't worry about the Domain Authority for YouTube Videos; you will get one automatically once you upload your own video to YouTube.

Ok great, now let me show you what I found by analyzing every one of the top

10 pages of Google under the "potty training boys" term:

Domain Authority: 86
Page Authority: 48
External Links: 6

Successful **potty training** for **boys** | BabyCenter
www.babycenter.com › Toddler › Potty Training › Potty Training Details
The key to **potty training** success is starting only when your son is truly able to do so.

Domain Authority: 82
Page Authority: 46
External Links: 5

How to **Potty Train** in a Week - **Potty Training** Tips for **Boys** & Girls ...
www.parenting.com/gallery/how-to-potty-train
Trust me, **potty training** doesn't have to be hard or stressful. Even as a first-time single mom with no dad in the house to help out, I managed to potty train my son ...
How to Potty Train in a Week - Best Potty Training Products

Domain Authority: 10
Page Authority: 21
External Links: 2

Potty Training Boys in 3 Days?
pottytrainingboys.org/
Jun 19, 2013 - **Potty Training Boys** Tips, Techniques, When And How To Start, Problems You Might Encounter, Recommended Books, Free Videos, And More.

Domain Authority: 100
Page Authority: 51
External Links: 9

Potty Training Boys made Easy - YouTube
www.youtube.com/watch?v=tscEmPltCol
May 30, 2013 - Uploaded by Tech channel
Potty Training Boys in 3 Days How to Guide: http://bit.ly/potty-training-boys Is your child ready for Potty ...

Domain Authority: 100
Page Authority: 47
External Links: 1

Potty Training Boys - YouTube
www.youtube.com/watch?v=KrRJn5JIN5s
Oct 4, 2010 - Uploaded by RNK Innovations
How to **potty train boys** using the Potty Training in One Day method and Potty Scotty products.

Domain Authority: 66
Page Authority: 29
External Links: 4

How to **Potty Train A Boy** - Scary Mommy
www.scarymommy.com/how-to-potty-train-a-boy/
parenting BY dummies is a humor, lifestyle blog written by the best mom in the world. In her free time she enjoys losing weight easily, looking like a soap star the ...

Domain Authority: 84
Page Authority: 43
External Links: 3

Potty Training Tips for **Boys** - Parents
www.parents.com › ... › Potty Training › Potty Training Tips
Potty training boys can be tough! To the rescue: Jen Singer, author of the Stop Second-Guessing Yourself guides to parenting and Pull-Ups Potty Training ...

Domain Authority: 64
Page Authority: 26
External Links: 1

Potty training for **boys** - BabyCentre
www.babycentre.co.uk/a548955/potty-training-for-boys
A complete guide to **potty training** your son. - BabyCentre.

Domain Authority: 83
Page Authority: 30
External Links: 0

Easy Ways to **Potty Train Boys** - Moms - Popsugar
moms.popsugar.com/Easy-Ways-Potty-Train-Boys-27330399
Mar 23, 2013 - Although many potty-training tips apply to boys and girls alike, potty training boys does pose some unique challenges. Whether you're ...

Domain Authority: 99
Page Authority: 1
External Links: 0

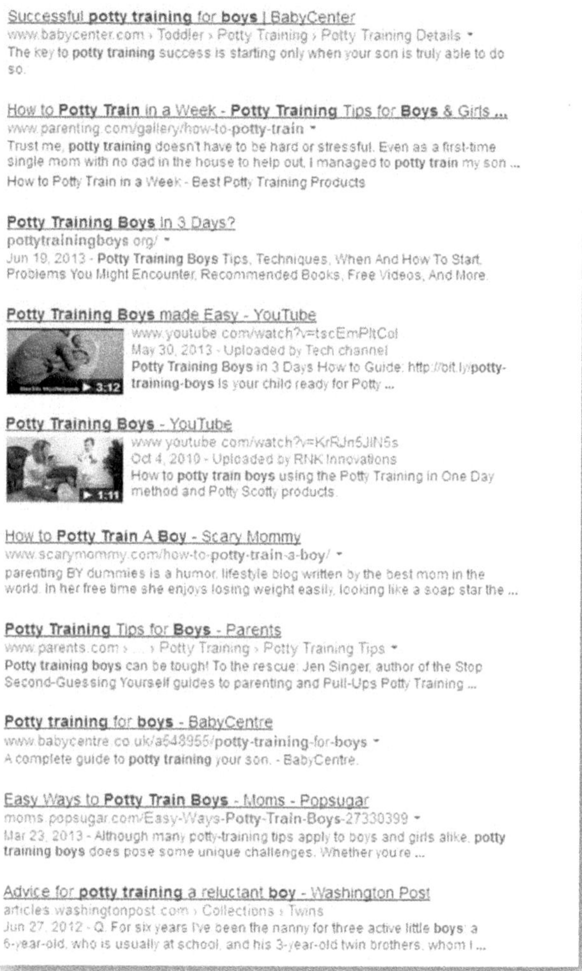

Advice for **potty training a reluctant boy** - Washington Post
articles.washingtonpost.com › Collections › Twins
Jun 27, 2012 - Q. For six years I've been the nanny for three active little boys: a 6-year-old, who is usually at school, and his 3-year-old twin brothers, whom I ...

There is absolutely a great chance to rank at the top of Google using this keyword. All of the pages are weak according to high quality backlinks; we may see that the 3rd spot is a really weak competitor and also we see there are 2 videos ranking in the top, which are weak also.

The 3rd spot is showing us something extremely important to get in the top, and is evidence that it is doing a better job than the URLs below it.

Potty Training Boys In 3 Days?
pottytrainingboys.org/ ▾
Jun 19, 2013 - **Potty Training Boys** Tips. Techniques. When And How To Start. Problems You Might Encounter, Recommended Books. Free Videos. And More.

This spot is way better optimized than the other 7 spots below. You can see the administrator placed the keyword in the Title, in the URL (buying an exact match domain, which is a lot more powerful than creating an inner page with the keyword) and the keyword is used at the beginning of the description text.

What we can do in order to rank at the top with this keyword is do everything this competitor has done plus build a lot more high quality backlinks at a natural pace; more on that in the Last step. This will definitely outrank this competitor, as well as all the others that are below it.

Remember, you need to be worried about the top competitors, not about the millions of pages that are below them.

Finally, here you see a list of the keywords and the number of weak spots that they have for us to rank our pages at the top of Google for every one of those hungry audiences waiting for us to satisfy their needs.

Audiences (Keywords)	Searches	Weak Spots
potty training boys	12.100	3, 5
potty training tips	12.100	8, 9
how to potty train a boy	8.100	9
how to potty train a girl	5.400	3, 4
potty training girls	5.400	3, 7
3 day potty training	4.400	3, 4, 7, 8, 9
potty chair	2.400	5
potty training in 3 days	1.600	2, 7
toilet training in less than a day	590	5, 6, 7, 9, 10
potty chairs for boys	590	8

This is something that takes forever to do manually. Keyword Funnel Software has the ability to do this process completely on autopilot and at lightning speed. You will be able to scrape all this data straight to your Excel sheet in a matter of seconds.

Keyword Funnel Software is completely optional, its free anyway, you can do all this manually, but this is an option for you to do all this automatically without wasting your time and effort in something that can easily be automated. To get access to the free version of Keyword Funnel Software click here

Any way, if you prefer to do this all manually please refer to the steps we have outlined in the guide and you are ready to go.

Now you are done with Step 3. This is absolutely enough for you to start looking for a winning domain name and to install your brand new website.

Step 4: Register a Domain Name... the right one...

A domain name will be the address of your website. It will be the place where all the URLs of your website will be attached to. It will be the most important identifier for every one of the audiences (keywords) you will be promoting to.

That's why it is very important for you to choose the right one. There are 2 approaches you can consider on picking the right domain name. The first approach is by using an exact match domain made of a keyword that you will be trying to rank at the top of Google.

The second approach is using a keyword that might target every one of the audiences you will try to advertise to at the same time. Here I mean a more general topic keyword.

The first approach will give you quick top rankings, but will be centered only in 1 audience in the home page. Your domain name is an identifier, a better way to show your brand to the public will be the second approach.

It will be just great if the keyword you pick happens to be a winning keyword that has a high demand and has accessibility to be placed at the top of Google and that may refer to a more general topic so you may target as many audiences as you want at the same time. This type of domains and websites is what are able to become what is called Authority Websites.

Let's give some thought on picking the best domain to work with. The following tips will be really great for you to be aware of in order to make the best decision.

This is one of the most important decisions of all in your Internet marketing journey.

- ✓ If you are building a website for your Company you definitely need to use the name of your company as the domain name, please be aware that long domain names are hard to remember and boring to read.
- ✓ Use the Google Keyword Planner to find a keyword that has a lot of searches. Most of those domain names are already taken, but you may find a few that are still available.
- ✓ If the keyword happens to have great accessibility to rank at the top of Google that's great, if not don't worry, the inner pages are what you will be trying to rank at the top.
- ✓ If for some reason you couldn't find an exact match domain for a keyword you really liked then you can just add a word before or after. Examples would be kidspottytraining.com which can easily let people know that the site will talk about potty training for kids and not for pets; or use howtopottytrain.com which is a very common keyword that a lot of people use to search for, specially the words "how to."
- ✓ The best domain extensions to buy will be .com, .org or .net. These are the best ranking domain extensions by order.

I have been using Namecheap.com for years and I have not faced a single problem with any of my domain names. They have great offers as well in some occasions.

I decided to register howtopottytrain.org because it was the one that was available. Now you are done with Step 4, let's register our hosting now.

Step 5: Setting up your hosting… cheaply and safely…

Now that we have the address to our "virtual home", it's time to get the land where it will be built on. That virtual land where we will store all the files for our website is called Hosting.

Being more technical, a web hosting service is an Internet service that allows individuals and organizations to make their website accessible via the World Wide Web. Web hosts are companies that provide space on a server owned or leased for use by clients, as well as providing Internet connectivity, typically in a data center. (Taken from Wikipedia)

In simple words they are the guys that store your website and are able to put it live to the entire world using your domain name as the address to get access to.

I like to separate domain from hosting because if I don't like the hosting I can just cancel it and still have my domain separated to plug it in with another hosting company. Domain transfers are really long and complicated. And sometimes hosting services offer really expensive domain name registrations and transfers.

Hostgator.com takes really seriously the statement of a 99.9% uptime guarantee. I have been using it for years and I just remember one day years ago that my site was down for global technical issues and it lasted just minutes to get it online again after calling them; something that with other hosting services I just sat down and cried waiting for them to resolve my issue. (Not actually crying, but being really angry)

If your intention is to create a website for your Company only you can use the Hatchling Plan, but if your intention is to set as many websites as you want (to make a lot of money online) what I suggest you to do is to get the Baby Plan option.

During the registration process remember to let them know that you already own a domain name. We will connect that domain name with our hosting account in the next step.

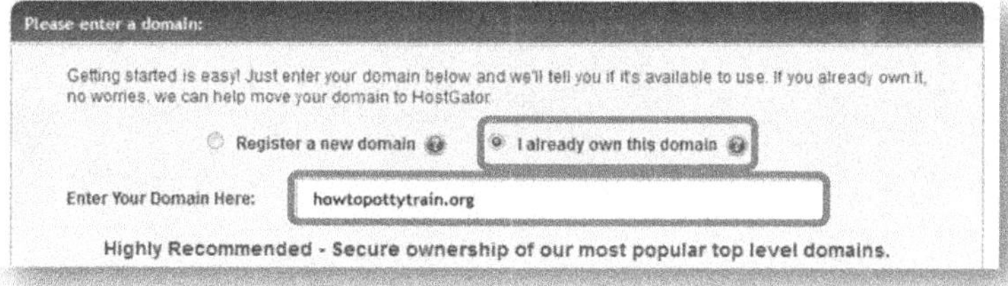

Now you are done with Step 5, it's time for you to create your SEMMM.

Step 6: Website Building... setting up your SEMMM...

Now it's time to create you Search Engine Money Making Machine and the process we use is the easiest one ever. We will use completely fre, but highly effective tools to create our website.

There are 4 principal components I will cover in this step. I will not waste your time with this, I know there are lots of these tools freely available on the web (especially themes and plugins) but I will show you what you really need for your site. Those vital components are:

1. **Add-on Domain**
2. **WordPress Installation**
3. **Theme Installation**
4. **Plugins Installation**

1. **Add-on Domain:** if you decided to buy your domain at namecheap.com and your hosting at hostgator.com now you will need to connect your domain to your hosting, and this is something that can take you 5 minutes thanks to the steps we will show you now.

First, you need to go to the email you got from hostgator.com telling you your Account info. Look for an email title like this:

With this information you will be able to enter into the Control Panel where you will find all kinds of awesome tools for your website.

What you need to do right now is to connect your domain to your hosting which is called the Name Servers.

Now you will login to your Namecheap.com account:

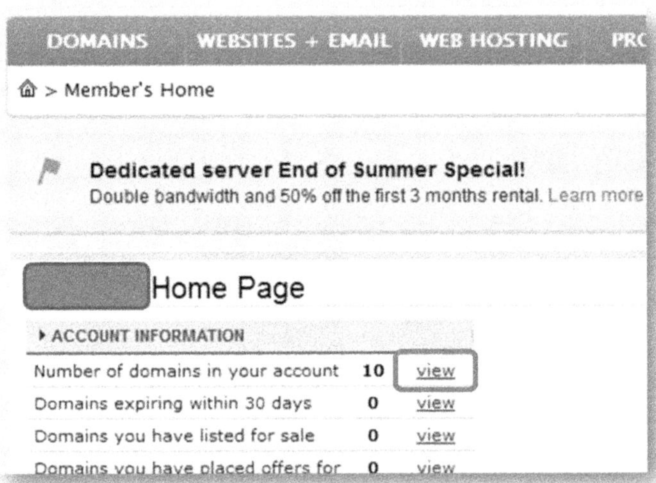
DOMAINS   WEBSITES + EMAIL   WEB HOSTING   PRC
> Member's Home
Dedicated server End of Summer Special!
Double bandwidth and 50% off the first 3 months rental. Learn more
Home Page
ACCOUNT INFORMATION
Number of domains in your account   10   view
Domains expiring within 30 days   0   view
Domains you have listed for sale   0   view
Domains you have placed offers for   0   view

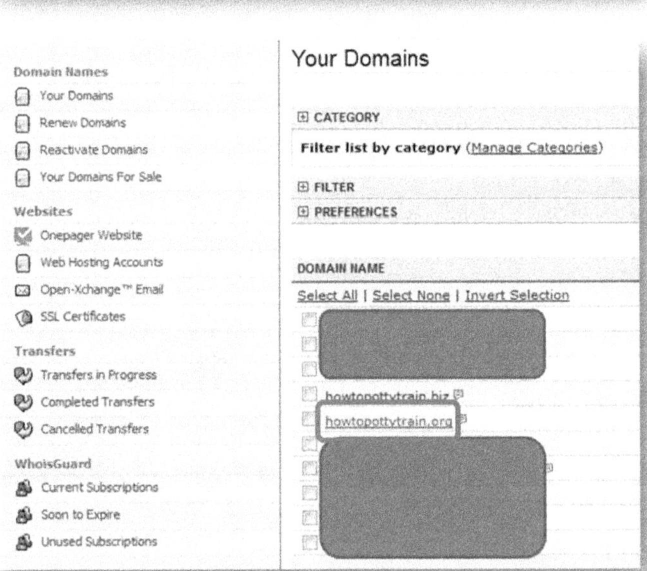
Domain Names
Your Domains
Renew Domains
Reactivate Domains
Your Domains For Sale
Websites
Onepager Website
Web Hosting Accounts
Open-Xchange™ Email
SSL Certificates
Transfers
Transfers in Progress
Completed Transfers
Cancelled Transfers
WhoisGuard
Current Subscriptions
Soon to Expire
Unused Subscriptions
Your Domains
CATEGORY
Filter list by category (Manage Categories)
FILTER
PREFERENCES
DOMAIN NAME
Select All | Select None | Invert Selection
howtopottytrain.biz
howtopottytrain.org

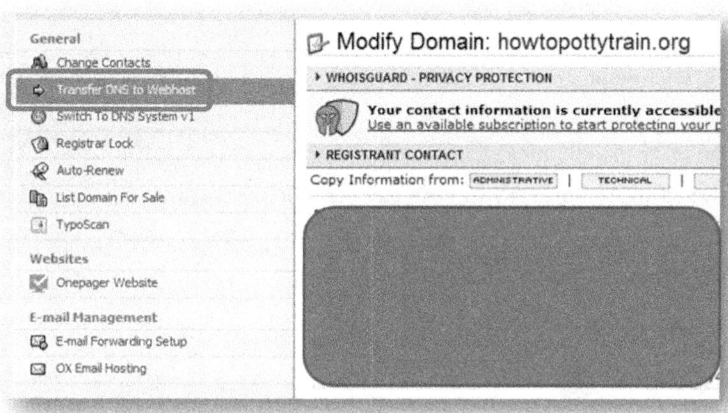

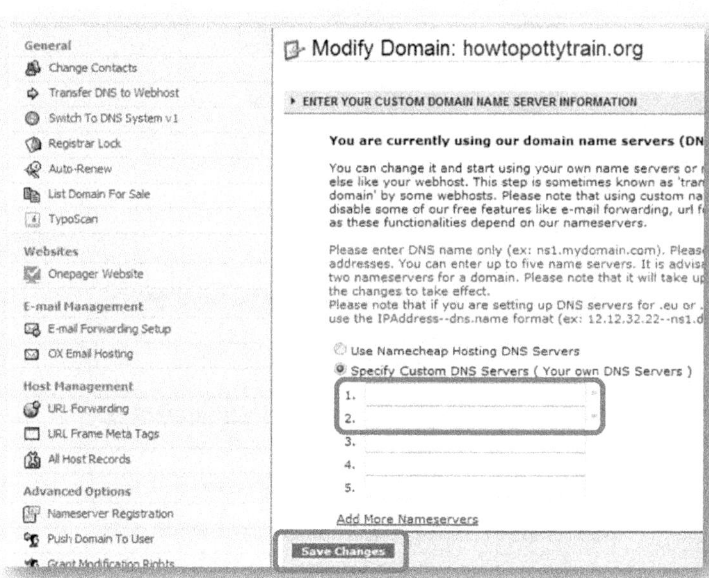

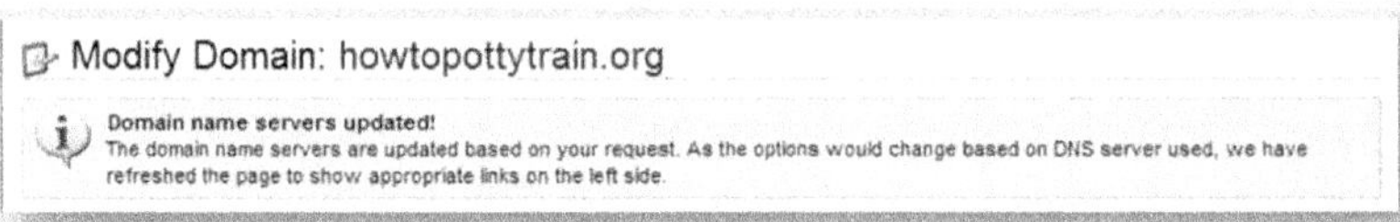

Now you need to login to your hostgator.com Control Panel:

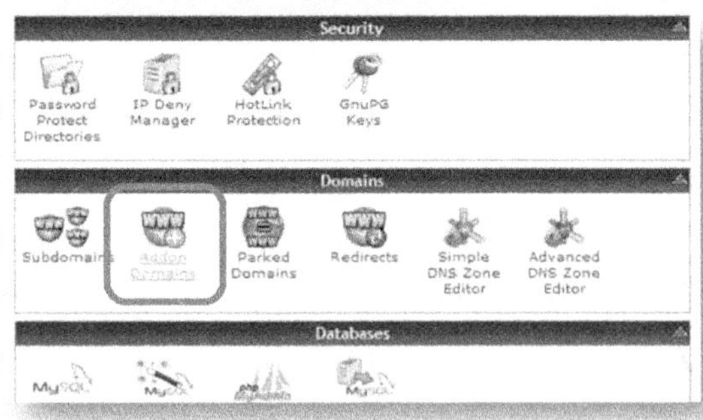

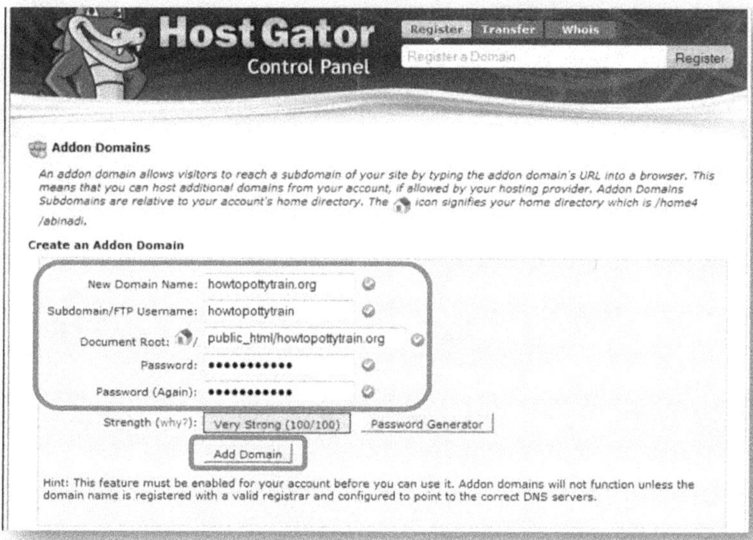

And there you have your domain name connected to your hosting in less than 5 minutes.

Now it's time to install WordPress to your domain, which is a lot easier.

2. WordPress Installation: if you decided to buy your hosting at hostgator.com you will use what is called "Fantastico De Luxe," so first go back to the home page of the your Hosgator Control Panel:

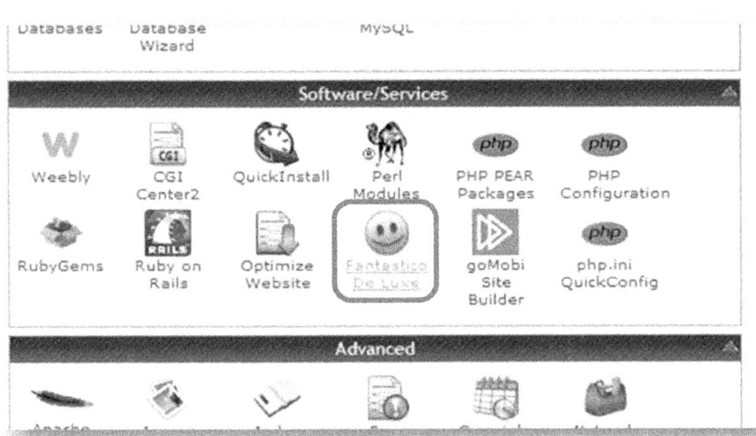

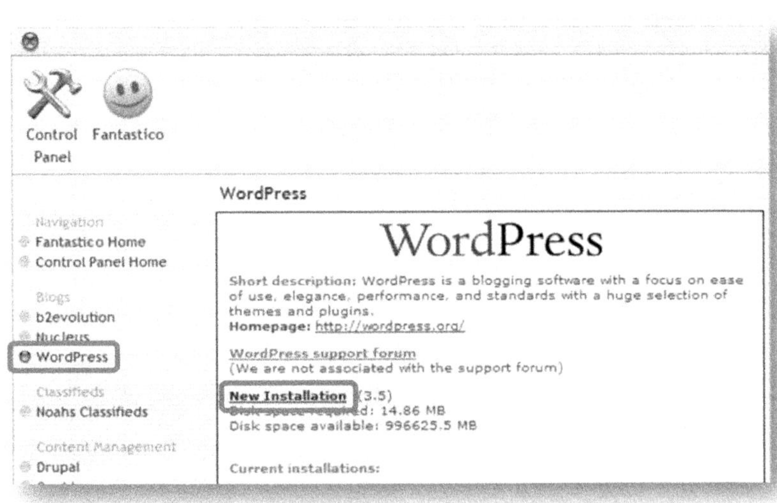

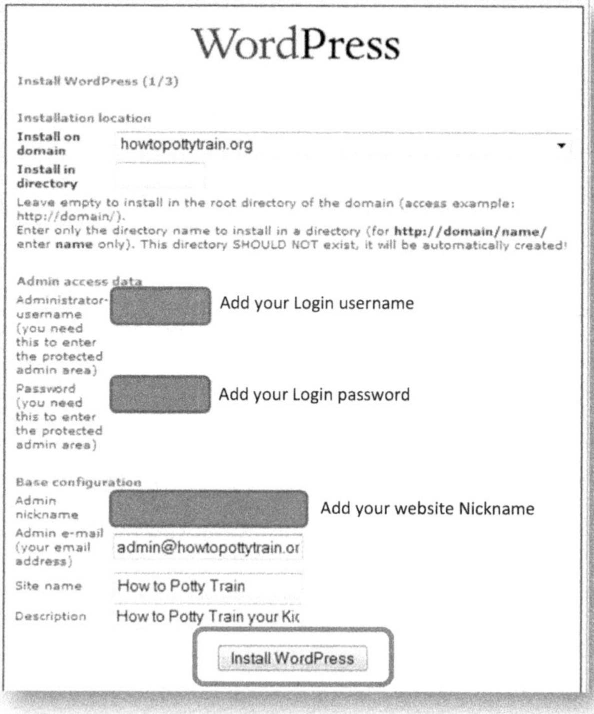

WordPress

Install WordPress (1/3)

Installation location

Install on domain
howtopottytrain.org

Install in directory
Leave empty to install in the root directory of the domain (access example: http://domain/).
Enter only the directory name to install in a directory (for **http://domain/name/** enter **name** only). This directory SHOULD NOT exist, it will be automatically created!

Admin access data

Administrator-username (you need this to enter the protected admin area)   Add your Login username

Password (you need this to enter the protected admin area)   Add your Login password

Base configuration

Admin nickname   Add your website Nickname

Admin e-mail (your email address)   admin@howtopottytrain.or

Site name   How to Potty Train

Description   How to Potty Train your Kic

[Install WordPress]

Install WordPress (2/3)

The MySQL database and MySQL user **abinadi_wrdp6** will be created and used for this installation.

- You chose to install in the main directory of the domain howtopottytrain.org.
- The access URL will be: http://howtopottytrain.org/.

Click on Finish installation to continue.

[Finish installation]

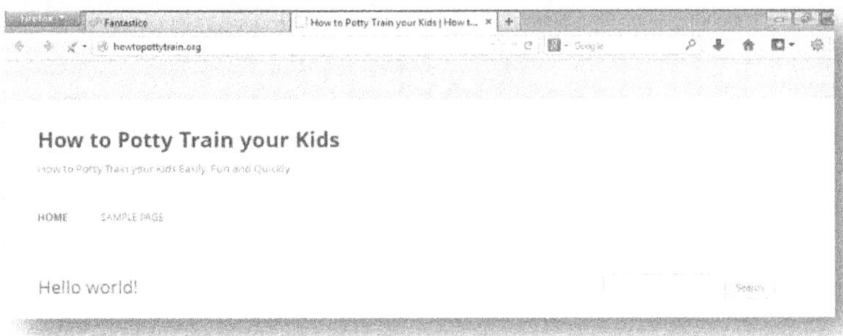

And there you have your WordPress site created quickly and easily.

Now it's time to install a theme for your brand new WordPress site.

3. Theme Installation: the following theme is a really nice one that will surely help you achieve what you want with your site. It is free as well.

http://www.s5themes.com/theme/simplo/

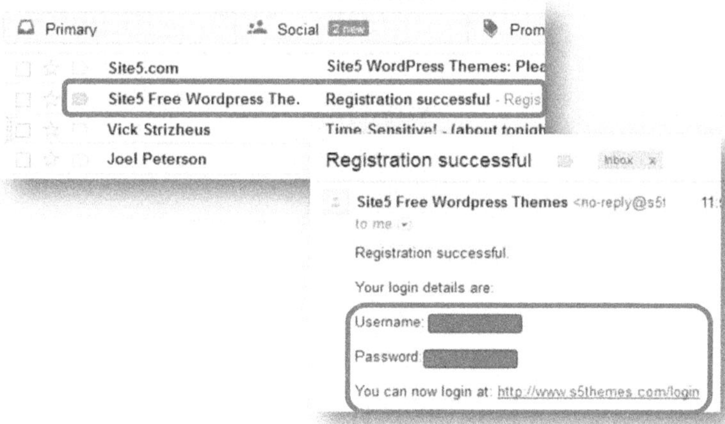
Simplo
Simple and clean blog theme coming with 6 color styles.
VIEW DEMO
DOWNLOAD
SHARE IT!
VERSION 1.0.0 | CHANGELOG | DOCUMENTATION | SUPPORT FORUM
Create New Account
Username
Email address
Subscribe to our newsletter too! Why?
REGISTER
Primary
Social
Prom
Site5.com
Site5 WordPress Themes: Plea
Site5 Free Wordpress The.
Registration successful - Regis
Vick Strizheus
Time Sensitive! - (about tonigh
Joel Peterson
Registration successful
Inbox x
Site5 Free Wordpress Themes <no-reply@s5t
11:
to me
Registration successful.
Your login details are:
Username:
Password:
You can now login at: http://www.s5themes.com/login

Go back to http://www.s5themes.com/theme/simplo/

Simplo

Simple and clean blog theme coming with 6 color styles.

◀◆▶ VIEW DEMO   ± DOWNLOAD   ⟨ SHARE IT!

VERSION **1.0.0** | CHANGELOG | DOCUMENTATION | SUPPORT FORUM

Already have an account

Username

Password

☐ Remember me

LOGIN

Forgot your password?

Simplo

Simple and clean blog theme coming with 6 color styles.

◀◆▶ VIEW DEMO   ± DOWNLOAD   ⟨ SHARE IT!

VERSION **1.0.0** | CHANGELOG | DOCUMENTATION | SUPPORT FORUM

Now we will log in to the WordPress Dashboard: yourdomain.com/wp-admin

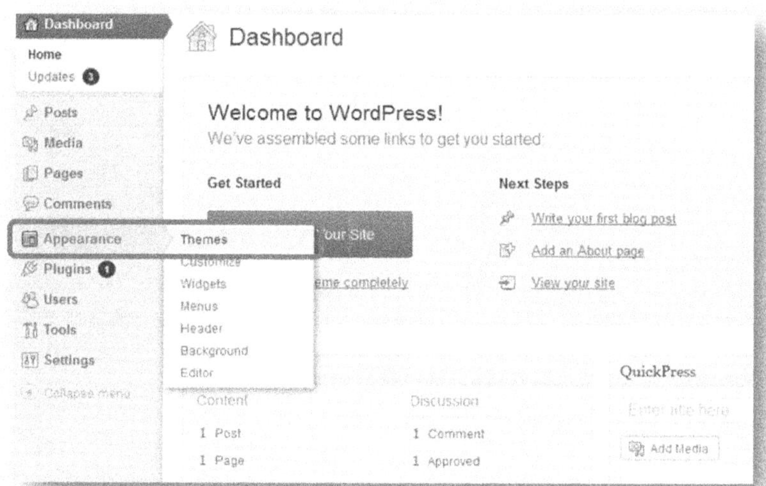

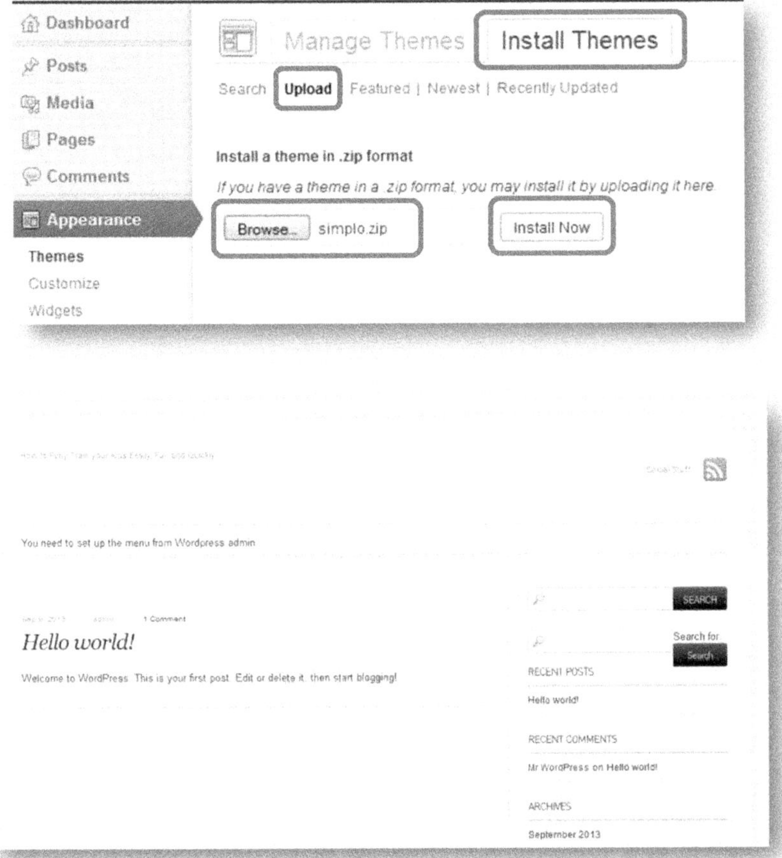

Now follow the steps below to insert your logo:

Dashboard
Posts
Media
Pages
Comments
Appearance
Themes
Customize
Widgets
Menus
Background
Editor
Manage Themes
Install Themes
Library
Add New
Visit site
simplo
Current Theme
Simplo
By Site5.com   Version 1.0
Simplo – Check Simplo Documentation
Customize   OPTIONS   Widgets

Upload New Media
Help
Drop files here
or
Select Files

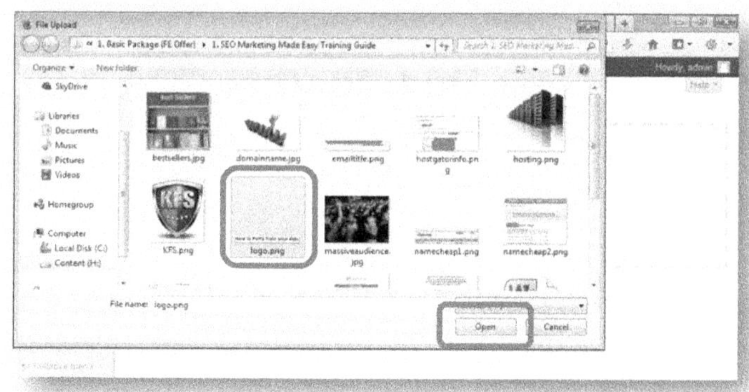

File Upload
1. Basic Package (FE Offer) 1. SEO Marketing Made Easy Training Guide
Organize   New folder
SkyDrive
Libraries
Documents
Music
Pictures
Videos
Homegroup
Computer
Local Disk (C:)
Content (H:)
bestsellers.jpg   domainname.jpg   emailtitle.png   hostgetorinfo.png   hosting.png
KFS.png   logo.png   massiveaudience.JPG   namecheap1.png   namecheap2.png
File name: logo.png
Open   Cancel
Howdy, admin
Help

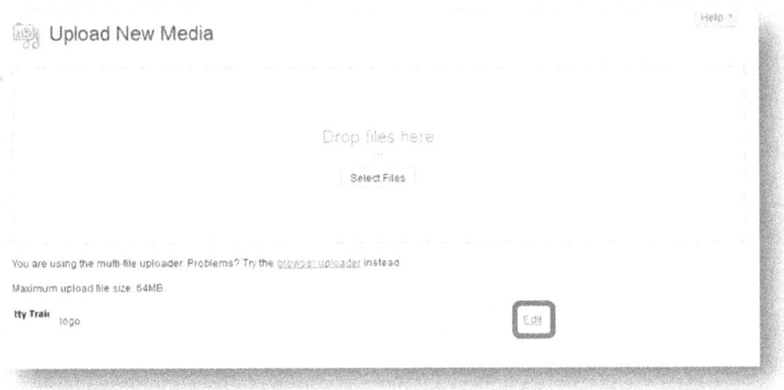

Upload New Media

Drop files here
Select Files

You are using the multi-file uploader. Problems? Try the browser uploader instead
Maximum upload file size: 64MB.

tty Train logo   Edit

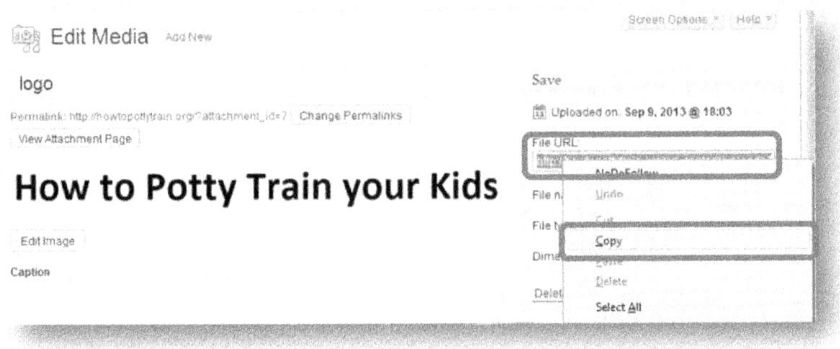

Edit Media   Add New

logo

Permalink: http://howtopottytrain.org/?attachment_id=7   Change Permalinks
View Attachment Page

How to Potty Train your Kids

Edit Image

Caption

Save

Uploaded on: Sep 9, 2013 @ 18:03

File URL

NoDoFollow
File n   Undo
File N   Cut
           Copy
Dime   Paste
           Delete
Delet   Select All

Pages
Comments
Appearance
Plugins 1
Users
Tools
Settings
Simple Options

How to Potty Train

Edit Image

Caption

Alternative Text

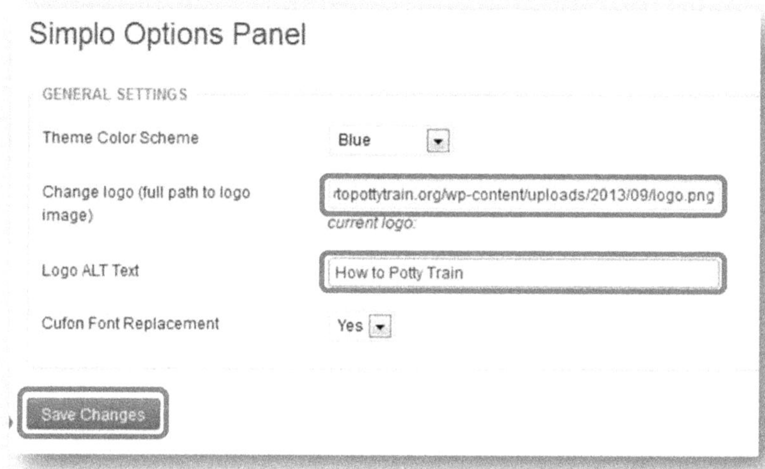

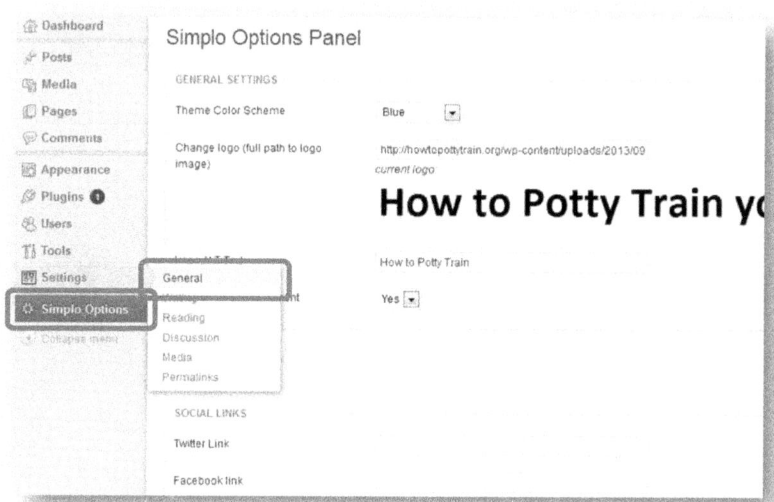

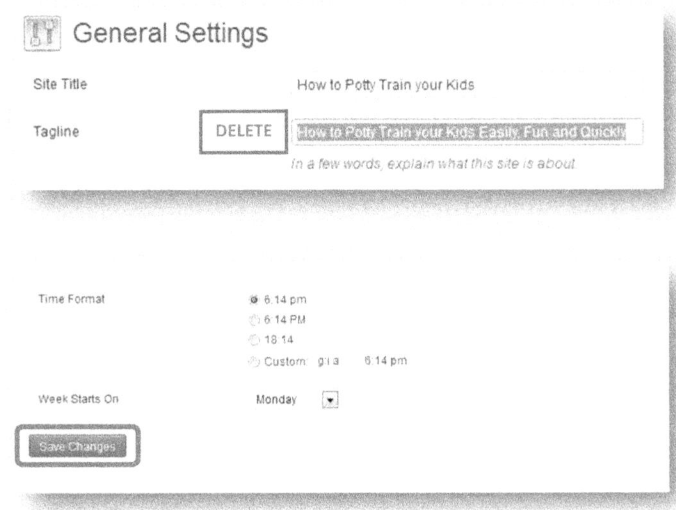

How to Potty Train your Kids

Now it's time to install some vital and highly effective plugins to your brand new WordPress site.

4. Plugins Installation: You are doing a great job so far. Now it's time to install a few necessary plugins or functions to your WordPress theme, and the great thing about WordPress is that everything is packaged into a small file that installs everything automatically so you don't have to play around with codes.

There are 6 vital plugins you will need to make your SE money making machine a lot more powerful:

Akismet: the best way in the world to protect your blog from comments and trackback spam. If you let people post spam content on your site, Google will notice that and it will hurt your ranking power.

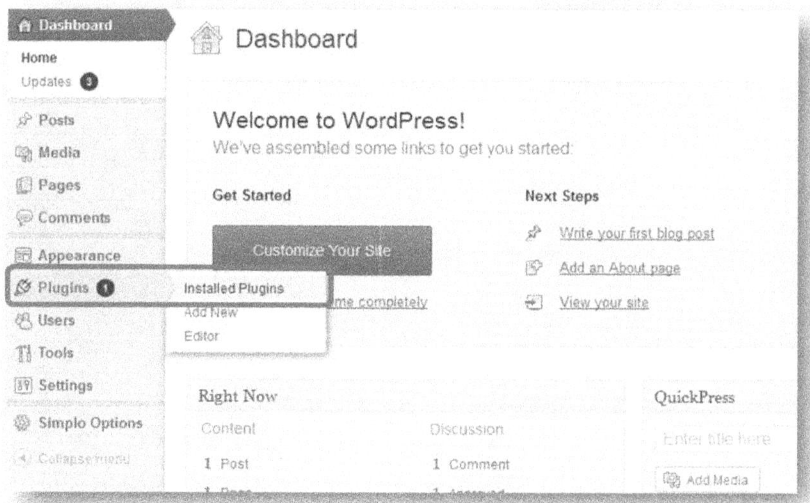

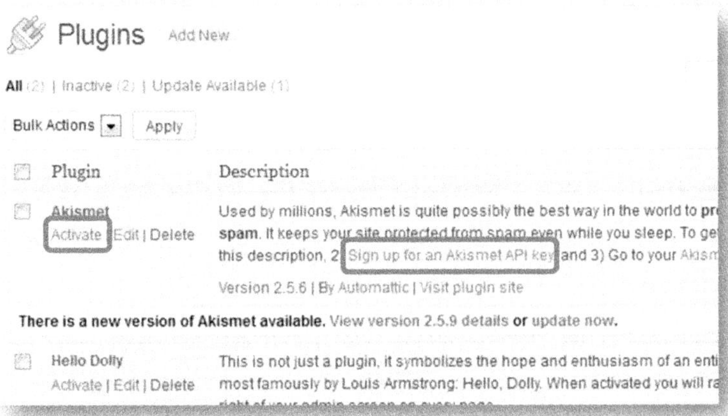

Google Site Maps: generates a special XML sitemap which will help search engines like Google, Bing, Yahoo and Ask.com to better index your blog

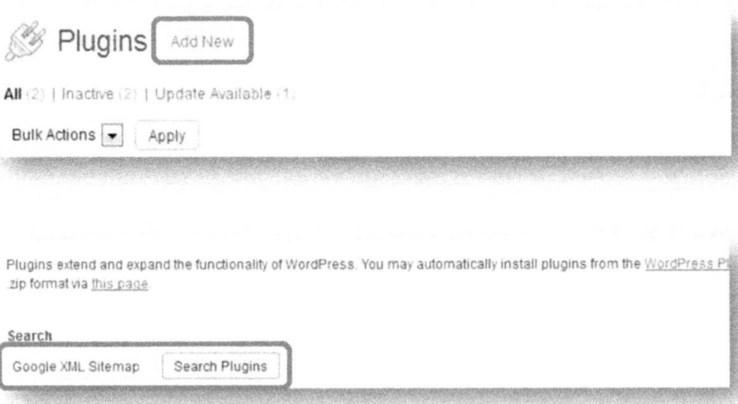

Redirection: manages 301 redirections, keeps track of 404 errors, and generally tidies up any loose ends your site may have. Google doesn't like strange URLs; we will use this plugin to clock and track our affiliate links.

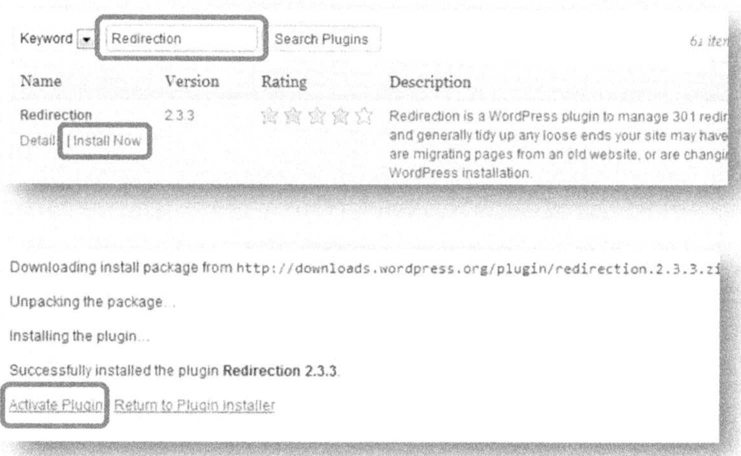

WP-Sticky: we would like to rank our home page for as many keywords as possible, that's why it will be a lot more productive to place all posts on the home page as well. This plugin will give you the ability to do this.

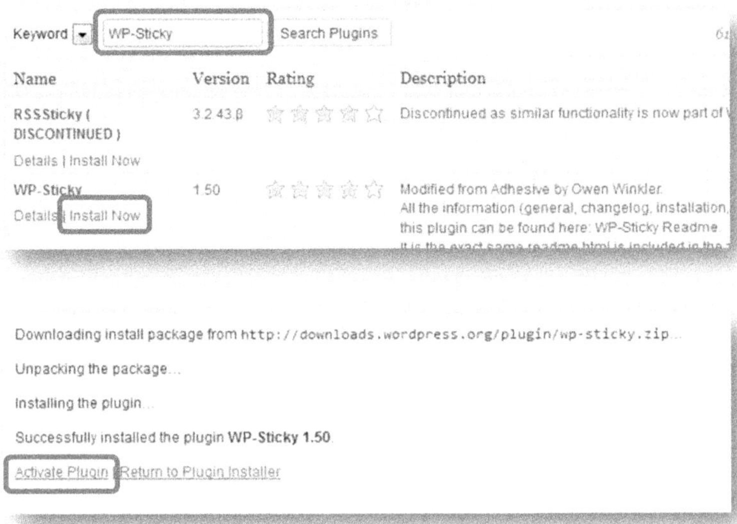

WP Super Cache: dramatically increases your site's speed by generating static html files from your dynamic WordPress blog. After an html file is generated your webserver will serve that file instead of processing the heavier WordPress PHP scripts, people love fast loading websites, that's why Google also loves it.

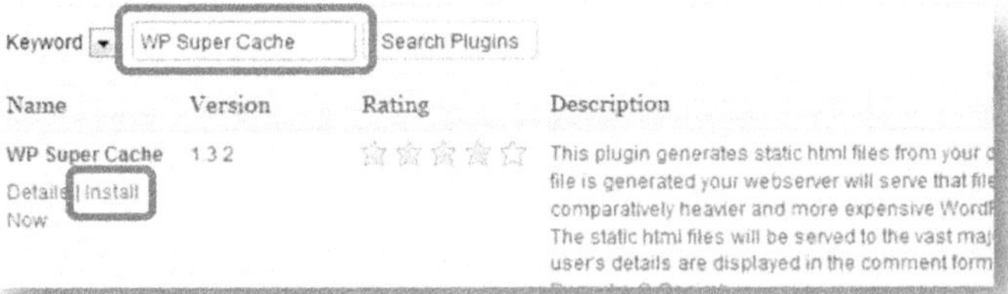

Downloading install package from http://downloads.wordpress.org/plugin/wp-super-cache.1.3.

Unpacking the package...

Installing the plugin...

Successfully installed the plugin **WP Super Cache 1.3.2**.

Activate Plugin | Return to Plugin Installer

All in one SEO Pack: efficiently optimizes your Wordpress blog for Search Engines (Search Engine Optimization).

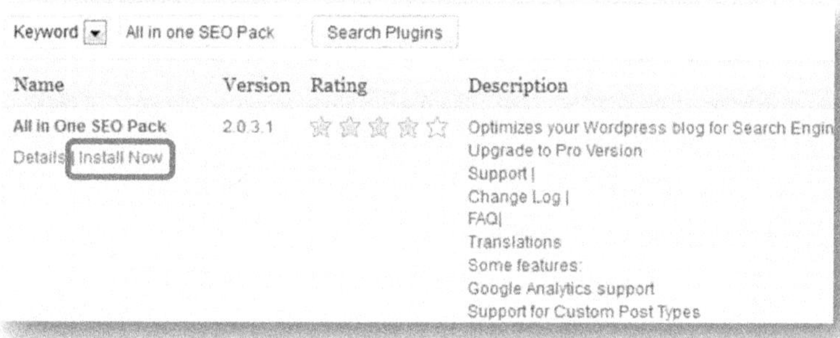

Name	Version	Rating	Description
All in One SEO Pack Details	Install Now	2.0.3.1	☆ ☆ ☆ ☆ ☆	Optimizes your Wordpress blog for Search Engin Upgrade to Pro Version Support	 Change Log	 FAQ| Translations Some features: Google Analytics support Support for Custom Post Types

Downloading install package from http://downloads.wordpress.org/plugin/all-in-one-seo-pack.zip...

Unpacking the package...

Installing the plugin...

Successfully installed the plugin **All in One SEO Pack 2.0.3.1**.

Activate Plugin | Return to Plugin Installer

We will optimize the plugins in the coming steps. Now you are done with Step 6, and it's time for you to create your High Quality Click-Magnet content.

Step 7: Creating Content... High Quality content please...

It's time for you to create your High Quality content that will effectively engage your visitor with highly helpful information that will satisfy their needs, as well as leading them to check on a better source like the product you are promoting.

The following tips will help you a lot to create some great content that people (and search engines) love:

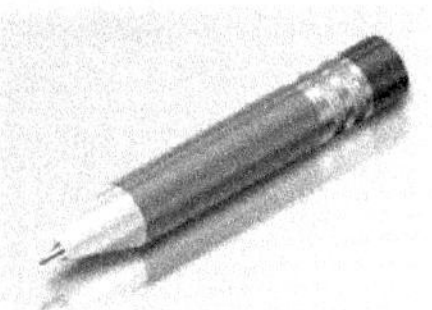

- ✓ An article should have no less than 800 words; the longer the article, the better. This will give a lot more value to the reader; this won't be a simple post for ranking purposes. This will help the visitor stay longer as well, and Google tracks that too.
- ✓ Forget about keyword density, focus on the content and not on how many times the keyword appears. Avoid what marketers do: putting keywords in places that don´t make sense.
- ✓ You need to make sure the content is of high quality, you have to dominate the topic, write updated content, proven tips, not old and spun content, if you decided to ask someone to do so just remember this.
- ✓ Divide the content using sub-headlines so people don't get bored once they see your webpage. Make it easy for them to see the principle ideas in the article in just a few seconds.
- ✓ Don't try to sell something, be helpful to them, and be neutral. People are looking for solutions to their needs, offer them something of great value but at the same time don't give them the whole pie. Just give a

considerable part of the pie and they will get the rest with what you will be promoting in other approaches.

✓ Obviously the article should be original. You need to make sure it is something that is not created by bots, coping and pasting online content and then hoping for the best. Of course you would need to do research, but then you need to write it in your own words and touch.

✓ Another awesome idea is to include images (check http://photodune.net for High Quality Images for $1) and a video right in the middle of the content, which will give a lot more value and will make the visitor stay longer.

✓ Place Links to other places of your website that might be relevant to the topic of the article, which will also help the visitor to stay longer.

✓ Finally, after you have given great value, in the last part of the content you can invite them to take this further and get access to something a lot more helpful. That will be your affiliate product and it better be even better than your content. You can include talking a little bit about the product, case studies, reviews, what people are saying, benefits, etc.

✓ If you are writing about a product directly, you need to give as much information about it as possible. Things like how old it is, who is the author, case studies, testimonials, reviews, negative and positive things, how to get access to it, deliverance method, price, special discounts, bonuses, invite them to buy and tell them why, etc. You should buy the product you are promoting in order to know everything about it, but please do not give away the content in your site or elsewhere.

In the resume you need to concentrate on creating high quality content for the reader instead of trying to rank on the search engine or to sell some affiliate product.

Forget about ranking in the top of the search engines, forget about making affiliate sales, you need to really concentrate on that audience, answering their questions, giving them a real solution, giving them value. That's what people want, that's what Google wants and that's what you should want.

There are other things we will do in order to make money with our site, but don't use the content to sell, use it to satisfy peoples' need. They will come back often because you offer quality, you offer a solution, you have what they need, they will trust you, they will trust your site and finally they will trust your recommendations as well.

What I like to do myself is to find great writers by going to odesk.com. This is an absolutely great platform to find high talented people in anything you need to build a highly successful business over the Internet.

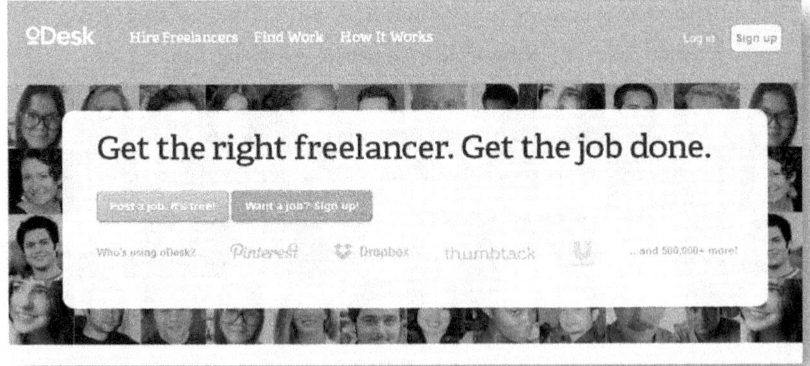

There you will find all kinds of great writers, all of them have their profile really well organized, and they can even show you their portfolio, as well as their quality and hourly rate. This is what I do to post my jobs there:

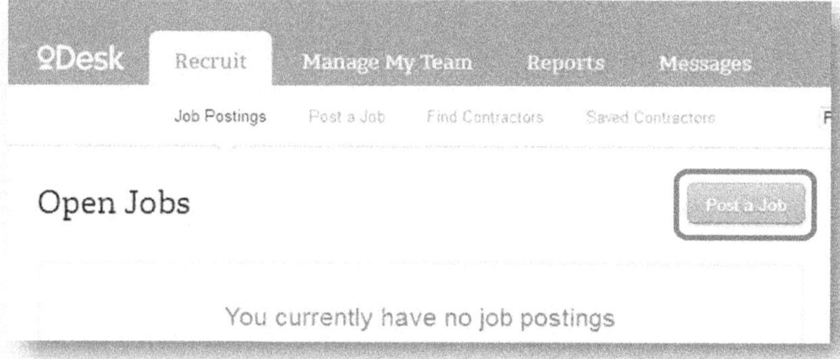

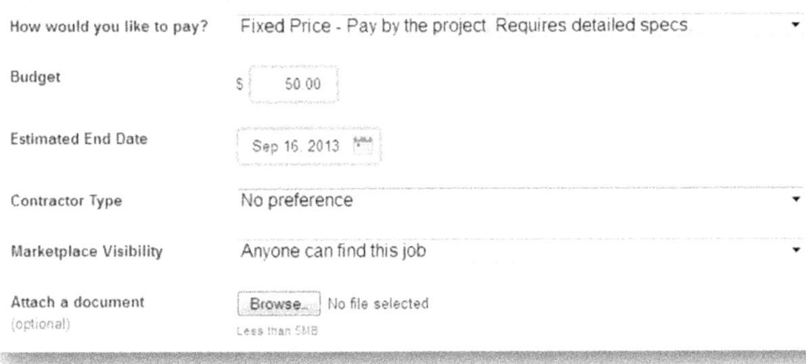

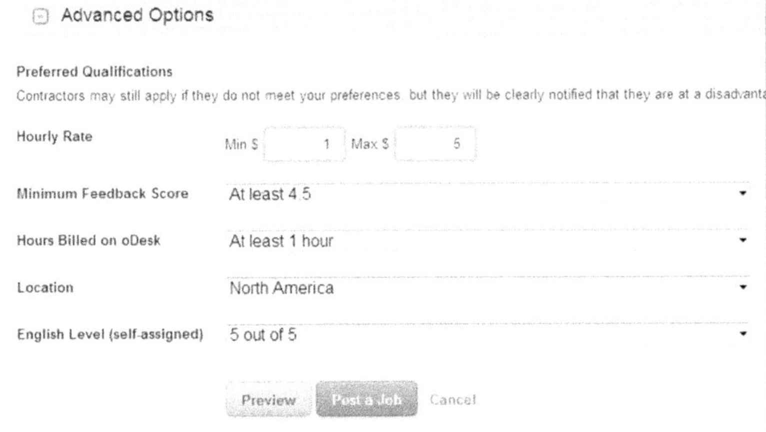

In order to find really high quality writers you will need to be able to pay a little bit more, but sometimes there are new people that can do a great job, and they charge a low hourly rate because they are new to odesk. You decide on that.

Another great way to find really awesome writers is on Fiverr.com. I found my writer there, and many Fiverr people are there to find clients and work for them off Fiverr (like in my case). You can get great results paying only $5 per article.

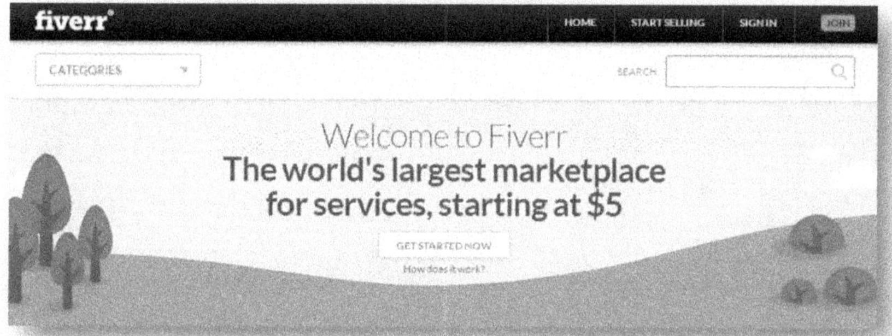

Right before submitting the articles to the website we need to apply a few SEO tweaks:

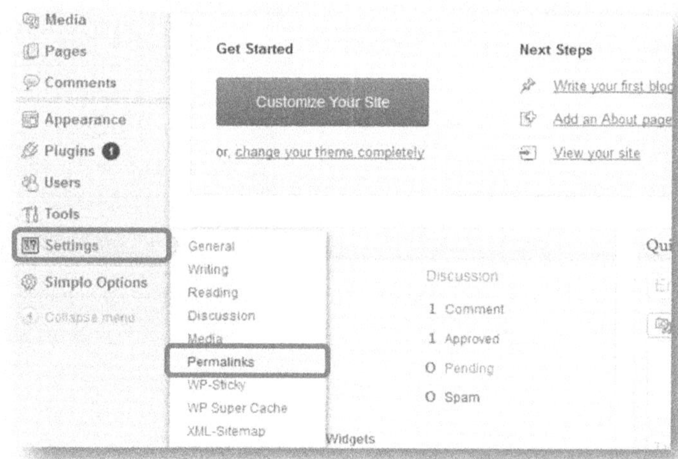

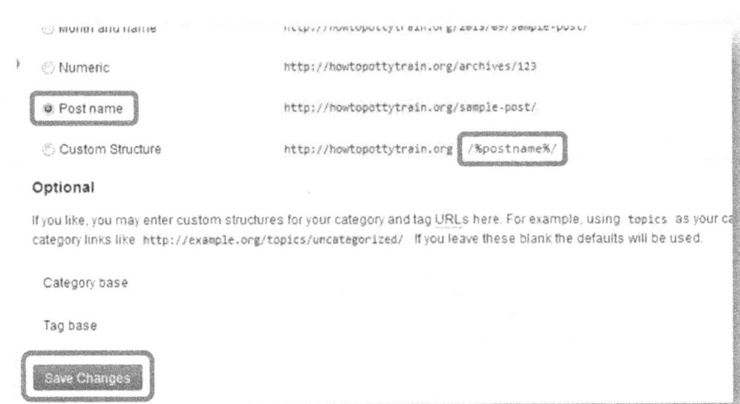
Month and name
Numeric   http://howtopottytrain.org/archives/123
Post name   http://howtopottytrain.org/sample-post/
Custom Structure   http://howtopottytrain.org   /%postname%/

Optional

If you like, you may enter custom structures for your category and tag URLs here. For example, using topics as your ca
category links like http://example.org/topics/uncategorized/   If you leave these blank the defaults will be used.

Category base

Tag base

Save Changes

Dashboard
All in One SEO

General Settings
Performance
Feature Manager

All in One SEO Pack Plugin Options

Join Our Mailing List

Join our mailing list for tips, tricks, and WordPress secrets.
Sign up today and receive a free copy of the e-book 5 SEO Tips for WordPress ($39

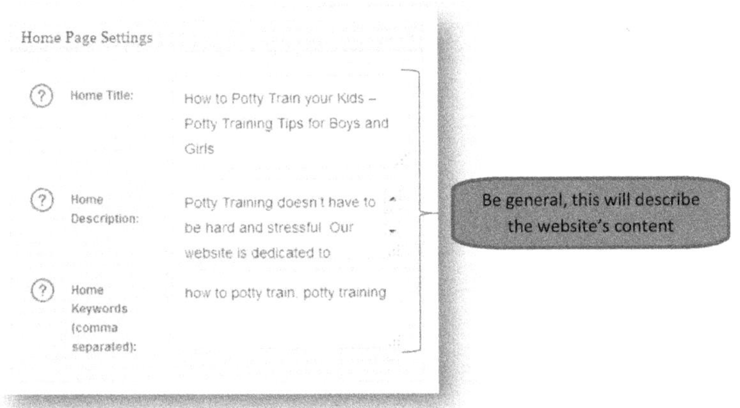
Home Page Settings

Home Title: How to Potty Train your Kids –
                   Potty Training Tips for Boys and
                   Girls

Home   Potty Training doesn't have to
Description: be hard and stressful Our
                   website is dedicated to

Home   how to potty train potty training
Keywords
(comma
separated):

Be general, this will describe
the website's content

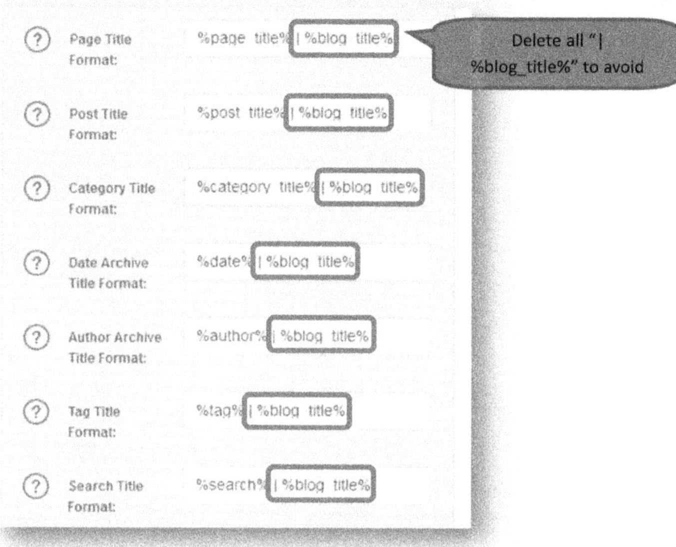
Page Title Format:
%page title% | %blog title%
Delete all " | %blog_title%" to avoid
Post Title Format:
%post title% | %blog title%
Category Title Format:
%category title% | %blog title%
Date Archive Title Format:
%date% | %blog title%
Author Archive Title Format:
%author% | %blog title%
Tag Title Format:
%tag% | %blog title%
Search Title Format:
%search% | %blog title%

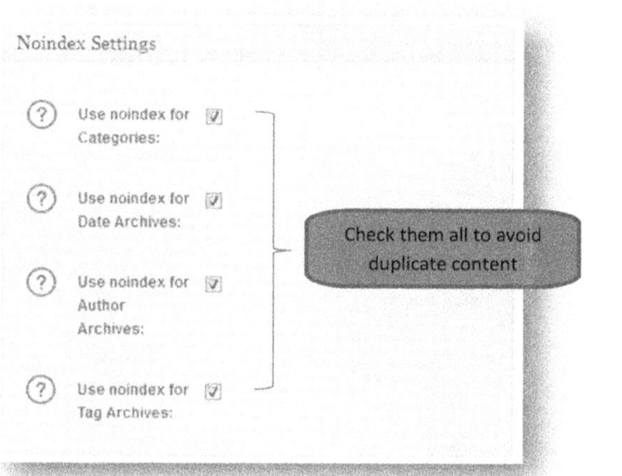
Noindex Settings
Use noindex for Categories:
Use noindex for Date Archives:
Use noindex for Author Archives:
Use noindex for Tag Archives:
Check them all to avoid duplicate content

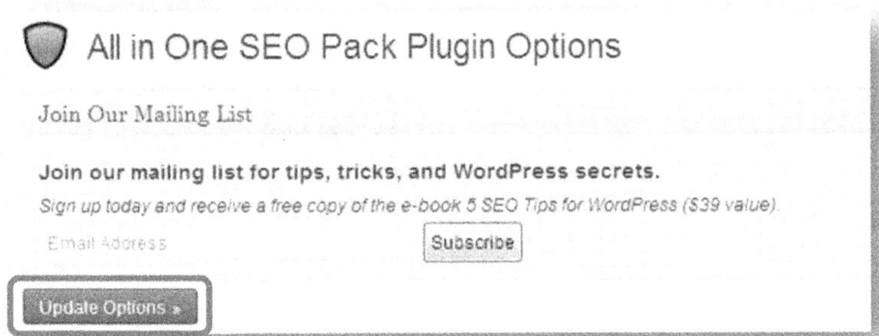

Now it's time to insert and optimize your content into your website. Let's create

our first post:

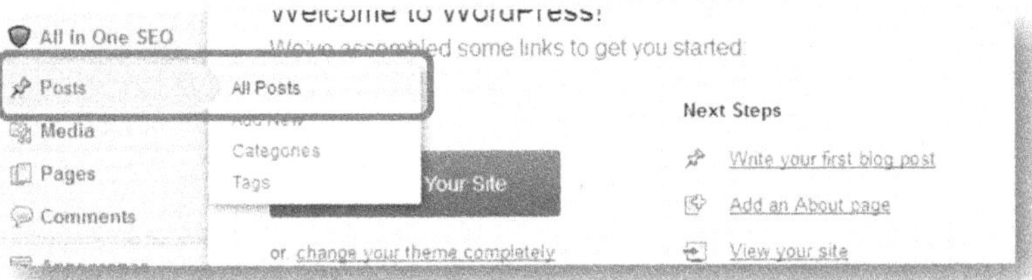

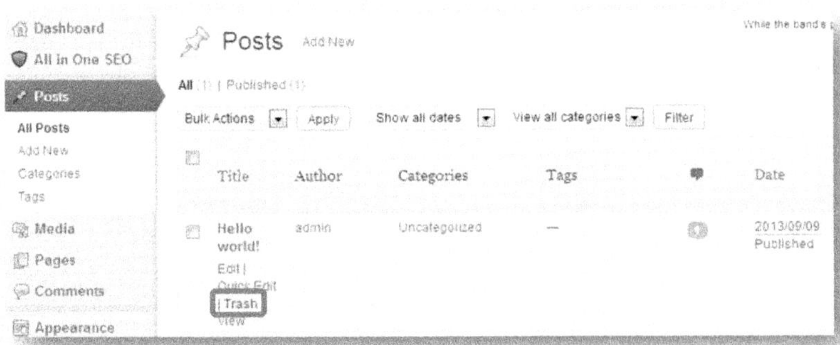

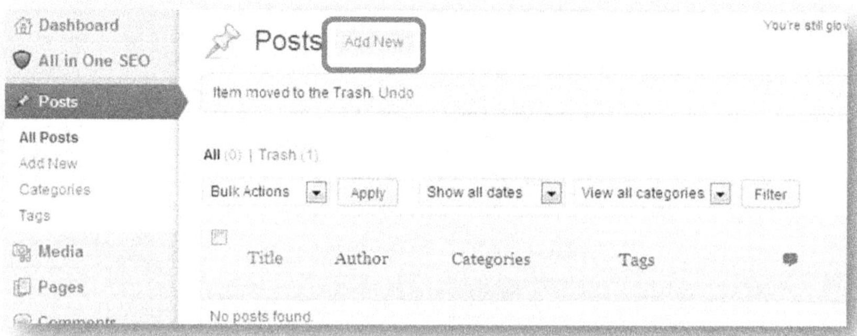

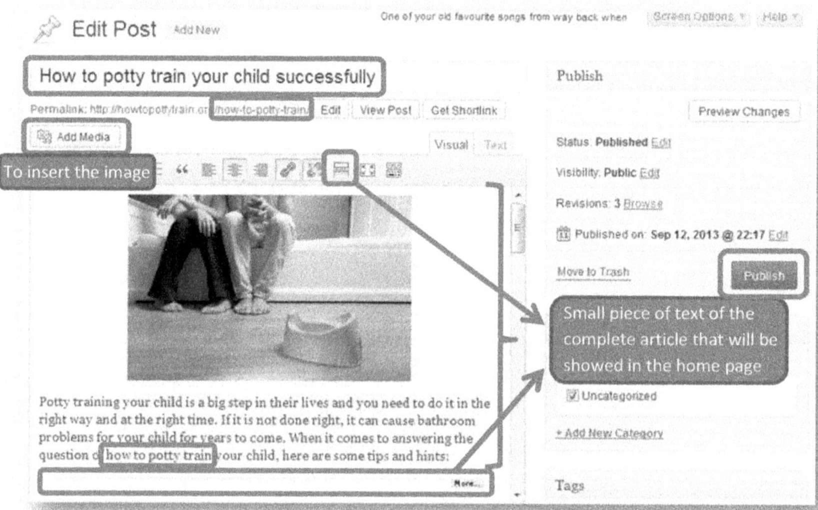

This button: ![ ] will divide the small part of the text before this symbol ![More...] that will be shown in the home page as an intro of the article. The original article in the URL http://howtopottytrain.org/how-to-potty-train/ will look like this:

And in the home page: http://howtopottytrain.org will look like this:

And here you will place the Title, description and keywords that will rank your page at the top of Google once people search for "How to potty Train."

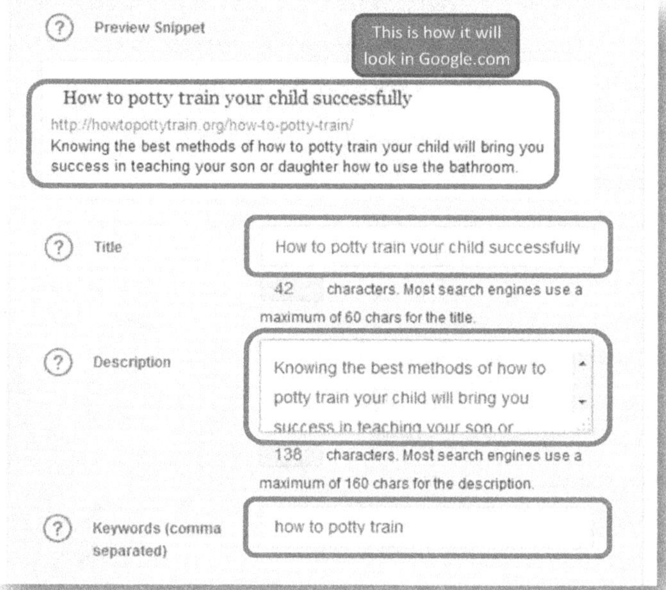

Remember to click "Update" every time you change something in the article:

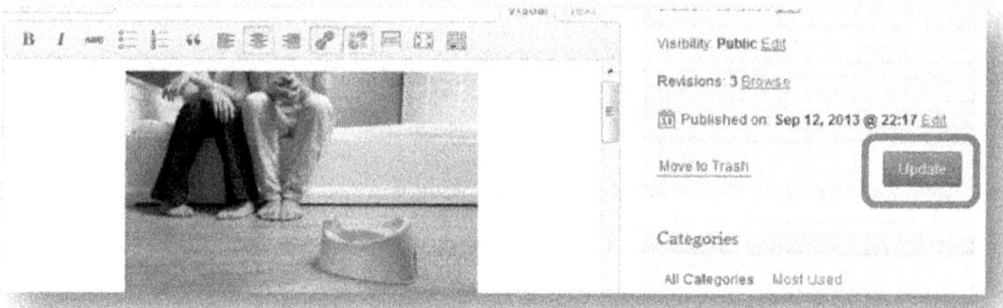

Now you are done with Step 7, so it's time for you to create your Click-Magnet Affiliate Connection that will get your visitors to convert into sales.

Step 8: Affiliate Connection... click-magnet technique...

Here I will show you some really great ways to connect your audience from your content to your affiliate offer. There are several ways you can use your blog to make money online. I will show you a few of the best ones.

It's true that you can do anything you want with your site, you can do wherever you want with the traffic that comes to your website (your audiences) but you have to be aware that the results you get will depend on what you do.

The purpose of your website is to provide high quality content, it is to answer people's questions, and for that reason if you buzz your webpage with a lot of advertisements people will think you just want to make money and probably your content won't be of high quality.

Of course you want to make money with your website, but you need to be really organized, adapt your money making intentions to the audience and place the right amount of banners in the right places. People go to content websites to find answers, they won't like to see crazy advertisements all over the place; they will like to see a really nice and well organized website with a lot of helpful content, as well as really nice and relevant tools (affiliate products) that might help them a lot more in the topic that they and you have in common.

Just be careful on how you treat your audience, don't think your website is yours, think your website is your audience's.

Think what information they would put in there; think what they would like to see in their website, think like a parent if you made a website that is parent related. Think like a person of the audience and don't just think like a marketer.

At the beginning of the e-book we noticed the Potty Training market was a great market to enter by looking at a high selling ClickBank product. That product will be the product we will advertise the most. But we certainly can advertise other products.

There are 2 principal places in your blog where you can easily advertise your products without disturbing your loyal readers. You can invite them to find a lot more helpful information at the bottom of the article and as well you can use all the right side part of your content to advertise products with really nice and relevant banners.

This depends on the subject your website is built on. The Internet marketing niche won't have that problem because those people are used to seeing advertisements everywhere. But with a topic like Potty Training, people will like seeing a lot of information more than advertisements all over the place.

A very important approach is to use a solution and not the greatest product in the world. Focus on banners that offer solutions to the problem matter. You must chose really nice images that may contain pictures more than just text.

I decided to show you 3 highly effective components for you to connect your audience to your affiliate offers and then to the money making potential of your blog. Those 3 components are:

1. **Call to action bottom content**
2. **Right side-bar banners**
3. **Link Cloaking and Tracking**

1. **Call to action bottom content:** for the call to action located at the bottom of the web content I decided to use a big image (to avoid duplicate content) that I will place in every page of my website. This is the image I will use with my website:

Want to Be Able to Potty Train your Boy or Girl in 3 days flat guaranteed?

Many parents who "never thought they could" have been able to do just that, with a popular "eBook" currently available called: "Potty Training In 3 Days."

The author Carol Cline, a mother of 4 children that she loves to death and who has been a daycare owner, wanted to share her personal history (2 years of experience) on how she stumbled upon a potty training method <u>**so quick and effective**</u> you can personally use it to have you child potty trained in just 3 days guaranteed.

A few of the books' success stories stated:

Followed your method to a "T" and now I'm happy to say my son is diaper free both day AND night for over a week now. This site was a blessing to our family!

Laurah Hamburg Jackson Hole, Illinois. September 11, 2013

I'm two days into your potty training method now and had to come back just to say that, it's just like what you said in the video, things started to "click" today. I'm pretty sure that tomorrow (day 3) my child will be fully potty trained! To anyone reading this, watch the video and follow her method!!!

Connie McDugless - Zurich, Rhode Island. September 11, 2013

Writing you here to say that I'm on my 4th day and my child Alisha has gone nearly 24 hours now using the potty on her own and without telling me when she has to go. Who knew I would stumble across this site and have a fully potty trained child 3 days later! I have liked this page and told my friends to come watch your video

Marcie Litman - Chance, California. September 10, 2013

This is the kind of book you might not necessarily find in your bookstore, but that an increasing number of parents are finding Kids Potty Training success with.

If you're looking to potty train your boy or girl in 3 days flat, and you're at that point of desperation, this might well be the best option.

<u>Click here to learn more about the "Potty Training in 3 Days"
program and how it can help you and your child.</u>

That image will be located below every article and that will be a perfect call to action to every audience that will be visiting every one of the pages of your website.

It will be great because they wont' see any advertisment disturbing their reading and after they have gotten their content they can finally see the offer right there below the content, as an option.

Go to the botton of the post and add the image:

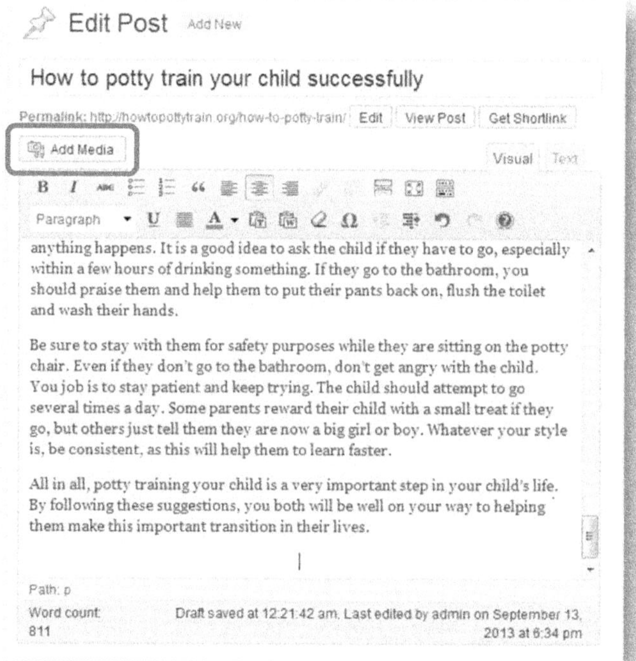

Remember to click "Update"

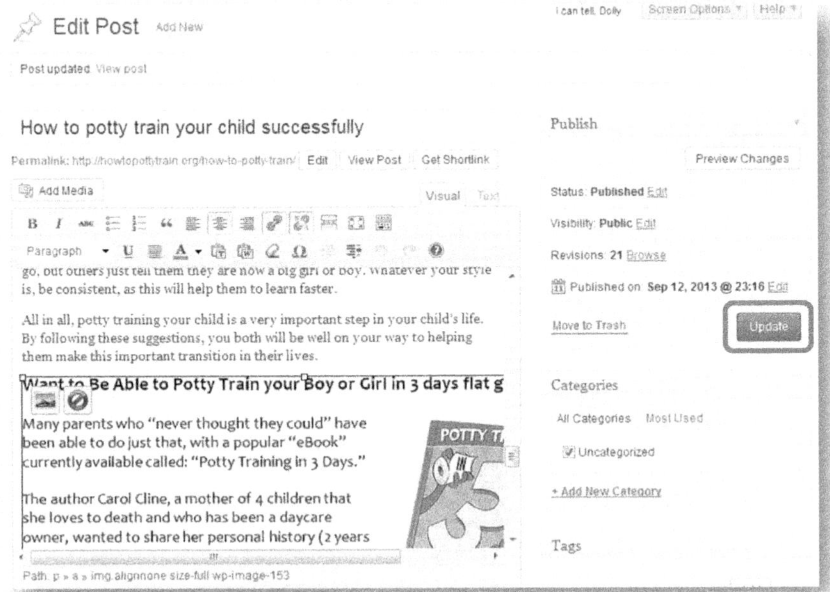

2. Right side-bar banners: this will be the 2nd place where you will advertise anything you want, but remember to be 100% relevant to your audiences.

There are a lof of things you can place here in order to advertise to your audiences, this place will be the exact same right side-bar that will be shown in every single page or post of your entire website.

What we are going to do here is to take everything unnesary from this area and leave only the most important ones as well as the marketing weapons we will use.

The marketing weapons we could use in this area are: banners, CPA offers, adsense ads, sign up forms, videos, etc. but the one I will show you now will be the banners, specially the Clickbank banners we will get from the Product we found in the first step of the process.

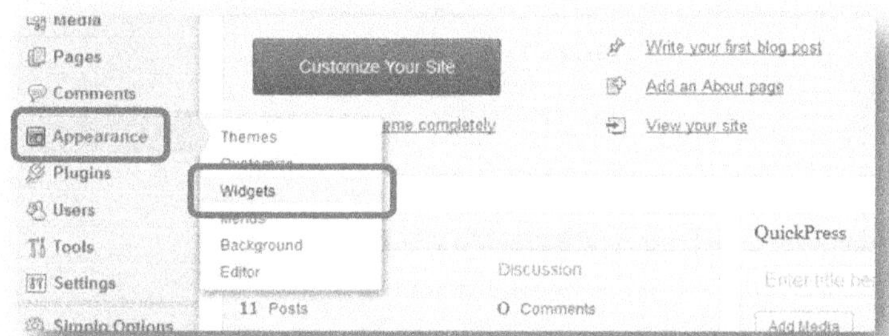

On the right side you will see everything is actually shown in the right side of your website. In the left side are all the tools you are able to use in that area:

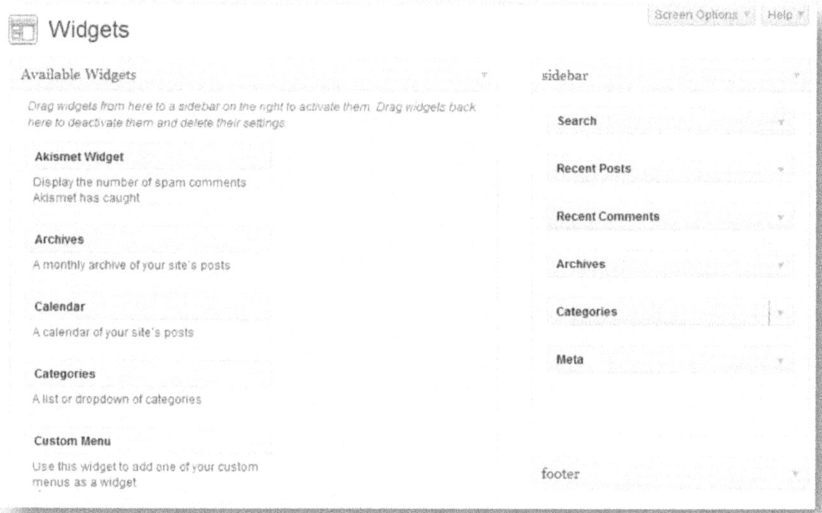

What you will do is delete every one, leave only the "Recent Posts" widget, set it up to 10 so the specific audience visiting that exact page may see all the content you have in your site.

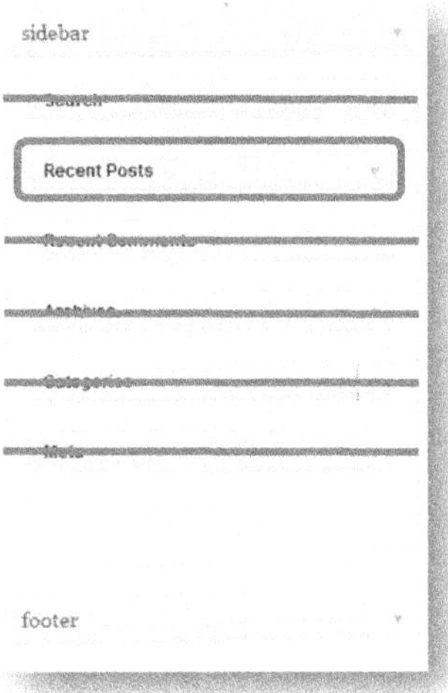

And then you will add the Text widget located at the bottom of the widgets:

You will need to click the left button of your mouse and holding the button you will drag it and place it above the "Recent Posts" widget:

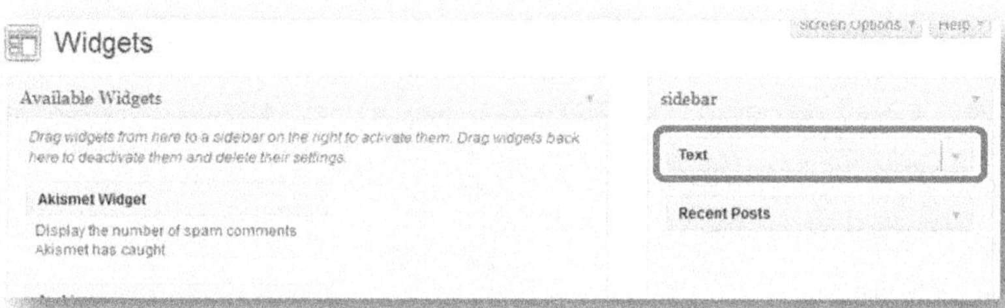

Now, we will insert the following code to the area and click save:

```
<div align=center><a href="http://YOUR-AFFILIATE-URL.com" title="Product Name"> <img
src="http://YOUR-IMAGE-URL.com" alt="Product Name" height="number of pixels" width="number
of pixels"></a></div>
```

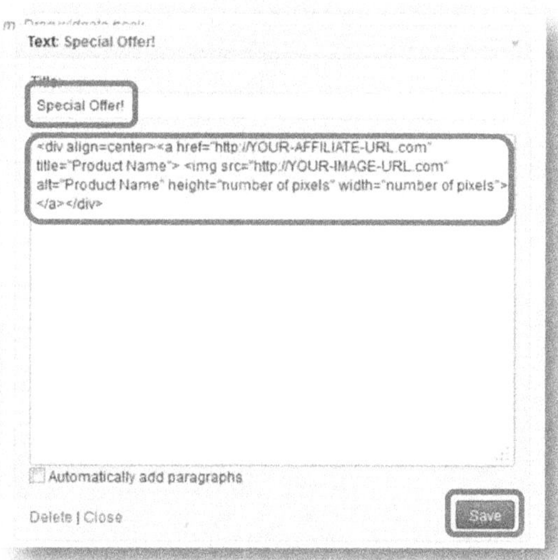

Now we will upload the banners we got from the product's affiliate area to our
Wordpress library:

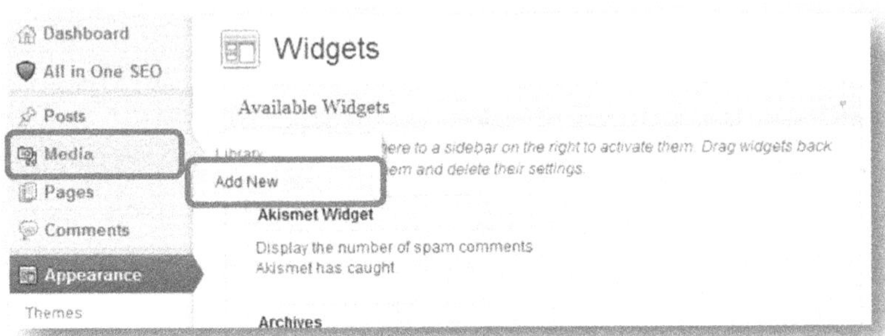

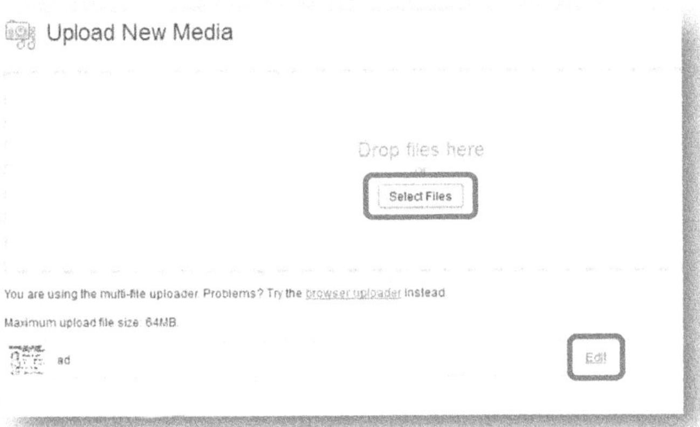

And finally we will insert the Affiliate link, Product Name and Image URL as well as the size of our choice in pixels and click "save."

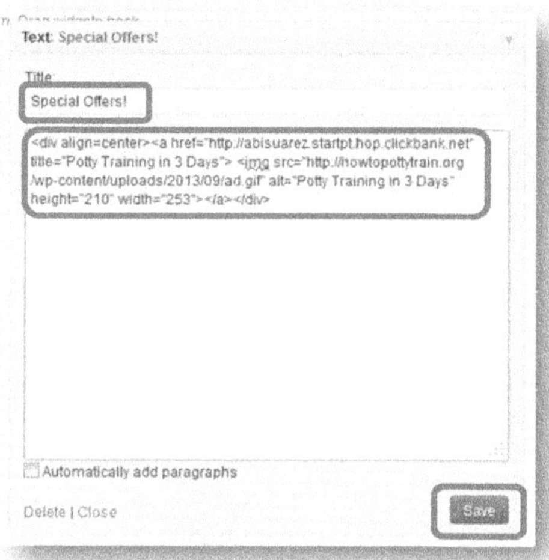

3. Link Cloaking and Tracking: this will be the way you will protect and track your affiliate links so you may have a record of what banners inserted in your site will give you the most clicks.

For this we will finally use the "Redirection" plugin.

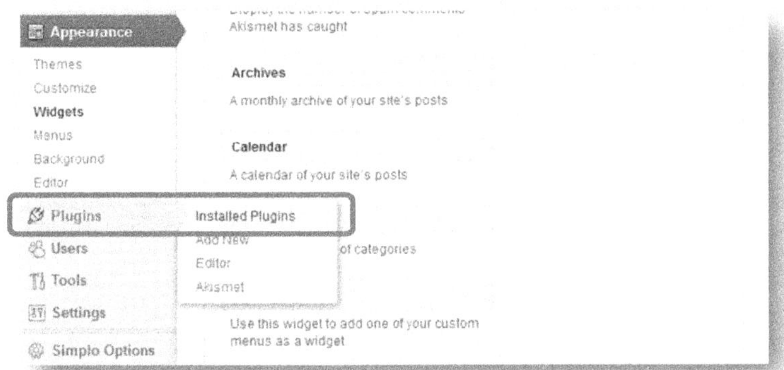

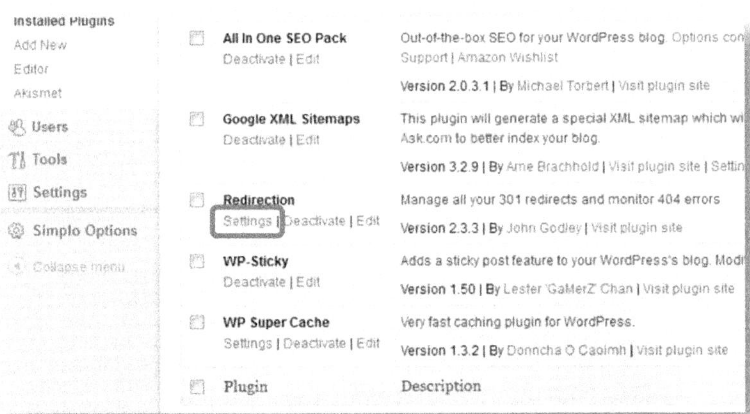

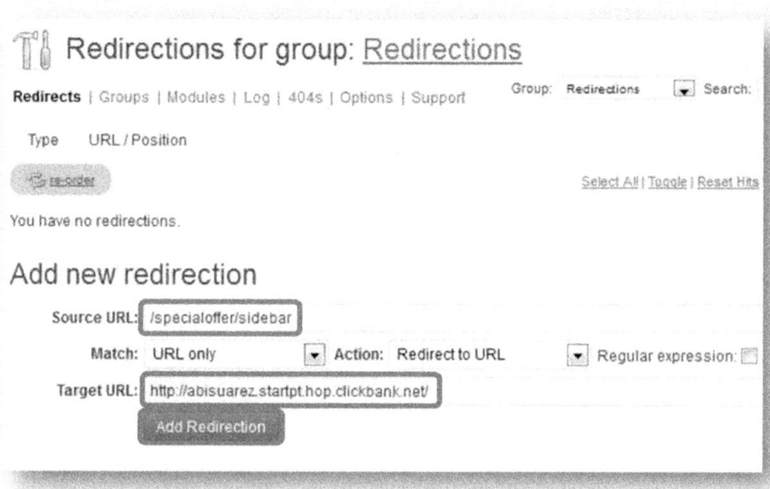

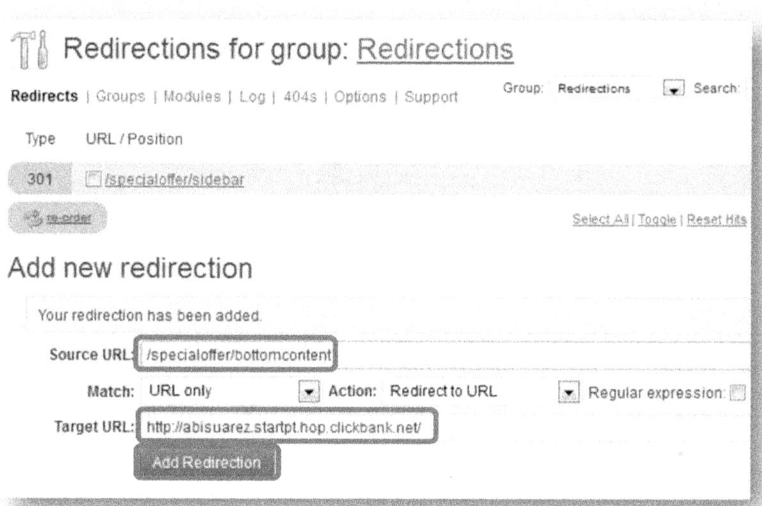

Now let's insert the new affiliate link to the images respectively:

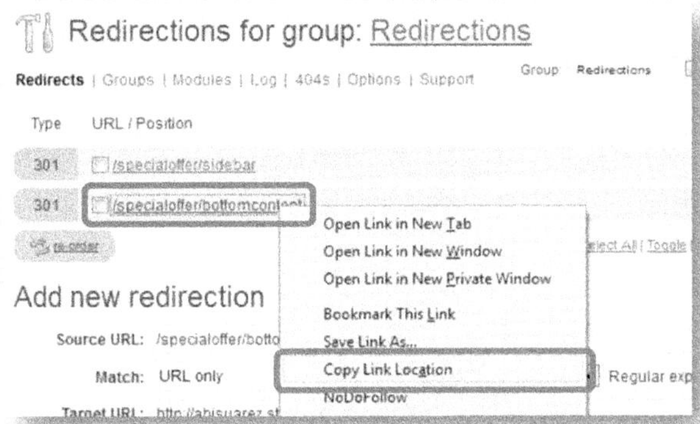

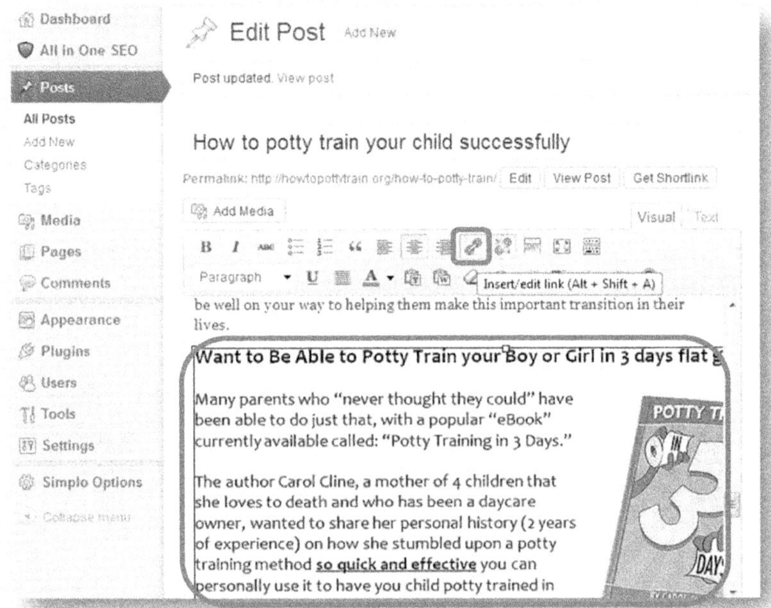

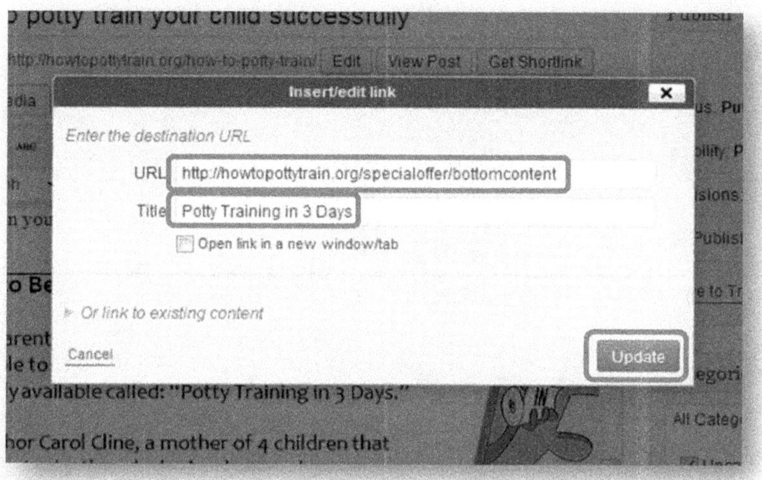

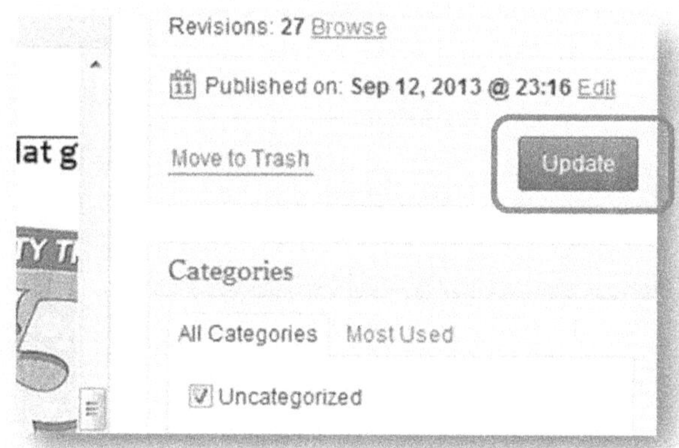

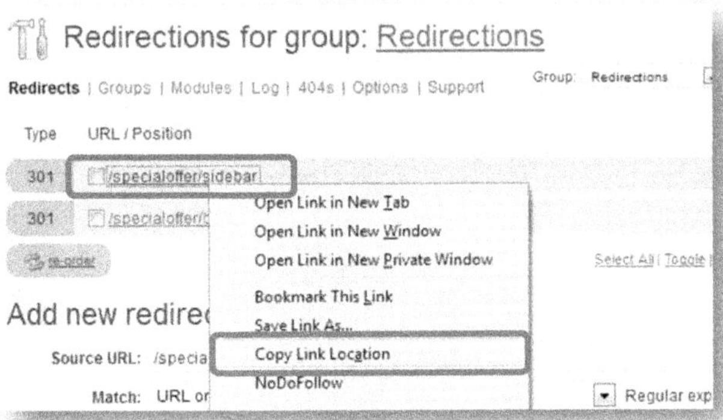

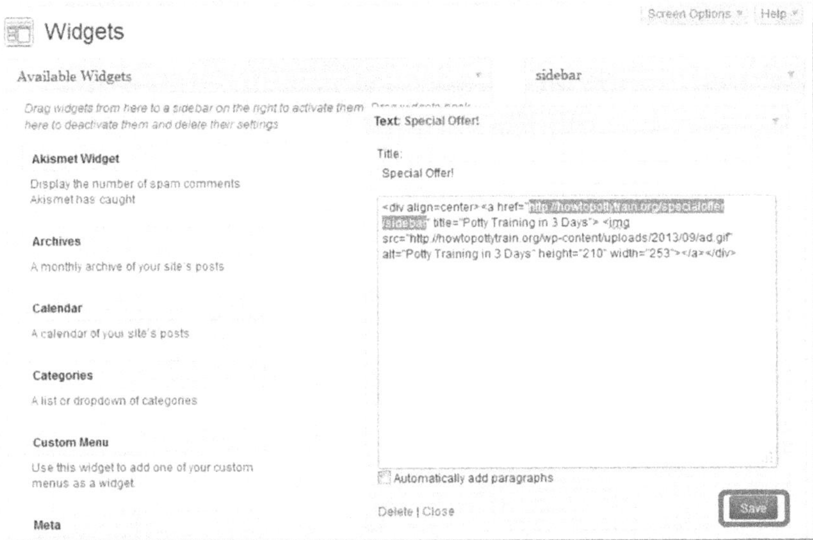

Now you are done with Step 8, do now we need to make some final highly

necessary adjustments to our brand new website to finish it 100%.

Step 9: Final Tweaks... absolutely necessary...

Now I would like to explain 4 really important things you must be aware of to include in your website, those 4 components are:

1. **Important Pages**
2. **Social Buttons**
3. **Copyright information**
4. **Google Analytics**

1. Important Pages: there are 5 really important pages you need to include in your website. Those pages are: Contact Us, Anti-Spam Policy, Terms of Service, Privacy Policy and About Us.

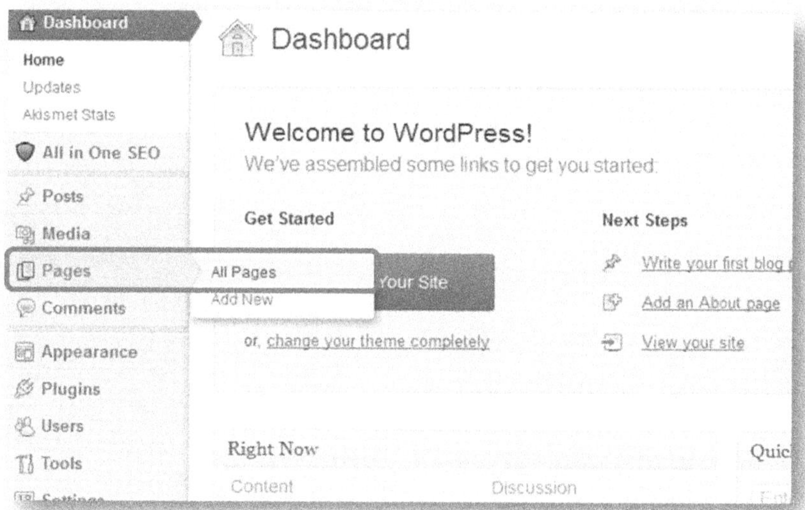

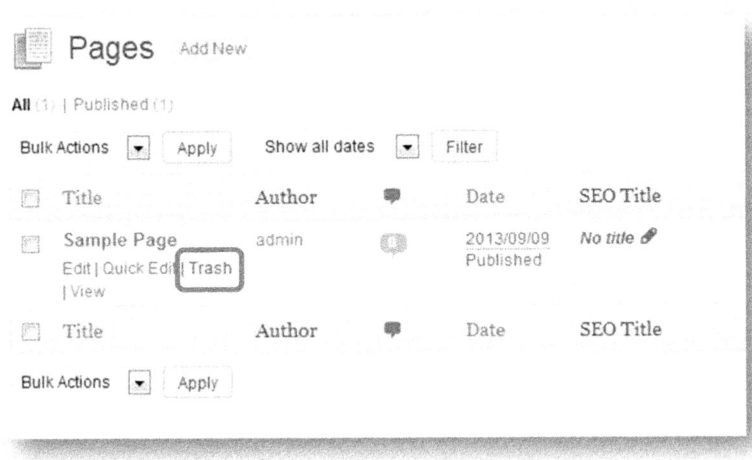

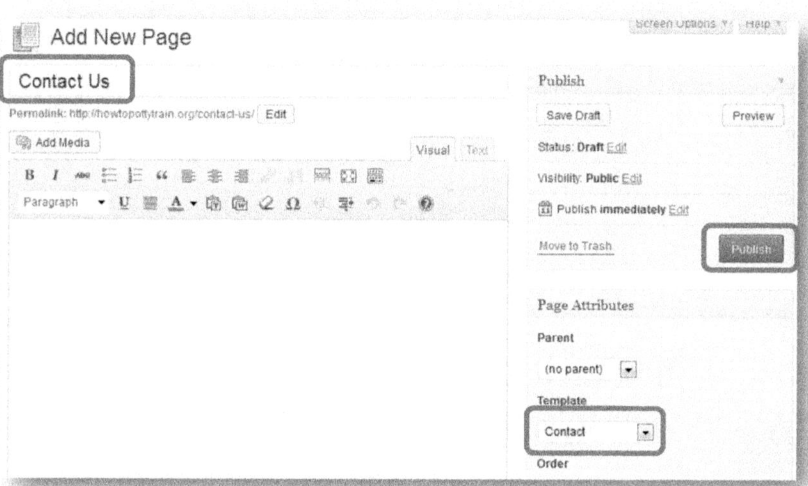
Add New Page
Contact Us
Permalink: http://howtopottytrain.org/contact-us/ Edit
Add Media
Visual Text
B I ABC
Paragraph U A Ω
Publish
Save Draft
Preview
Status: Draft Edit
Visibility: Public Edit
Publish immediately Edit
Move to Trash
Publish
Page Attributes
Parent
(no parent)
Template
Contact
Order

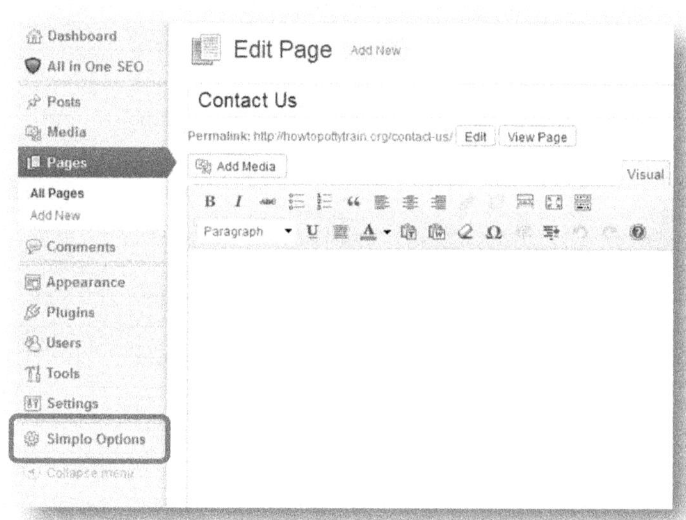
Dashboard
All in One SEO
Posts
Media
Pages
All Pages
Add New
Comments
Appearance
Plugins
Users
Tools
Settings
Simplo Options
Collapse menu
Edit Page Add New
Contact Us
Permalink: http://howtopottytrain.org/contact-us/ Edit View Page
Add Media
Visual
B I ABC
Paragraph U A Ω

CONTACT PAGE SETTINGS

Contact Page Text

if you need to contact us for any reason simply send us an email using the form
below and we will shortly answer you

Email Address for Contact Form

admin@howtopottytrain.org

Save Changes

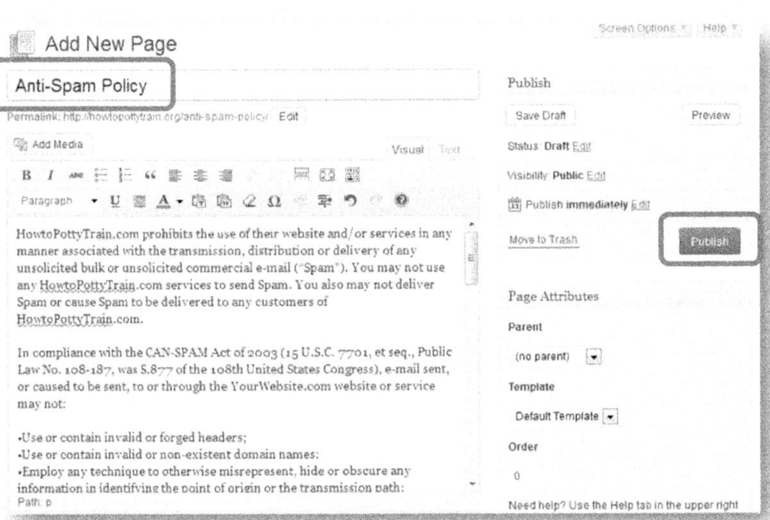
Add New Page

Anti-Spam Policy

Permalink: http://howtopottytrain.org/anti-spam-policy/ Edit

Add Media   Visual Text

B I ABC ≡ ≡ " ≡ ≡ ≡   ≡ ≡ ≡
Paragraph ▼ U ≡ A ▼ ≡ ≡ ⊘ Ω   ≡ ↺   ?

HowtoPottyTrain.com prohibits the use of their website and/or services in any
manner associated with the transmission, distribution or delivery of any
unsolicited bulk or unsolicited commercial e-mail ("Spam"). You may not use
any HowtoPottyTrain.com services to send Spam. You also may not deliver
Spam or cause Spam to be delivered to any customers of
HowtoPottyTrain.com.

In compliance with the CAN-SPAM Act of 2003 (15 U.S.C. 7701, et seq., Public
Law No. 108-187, was S.877 of the 108th United States Congress), e-mail sent,
or caused to be sent, to or through the YourWebsite.com website or service
may not:

•Use or contain invalid or forged headers;
•Use or contain invalid or non-existent domain names:
•Employ any technique to otherwise misrepresent, hide or obscure any
information in identifying the point of origin or the transmission path:
Path: p

Screen Options Help

Publish

Save Draft   Preview

Status: Draft Edit

Visibility: Public Edit

Publish immediately Edit

Move to Trash   Publish

Page Attributes

Parent

(no parent) ▼

Template

Default Template ▼

Order

0

Need help? Use the Help tab in the upper right

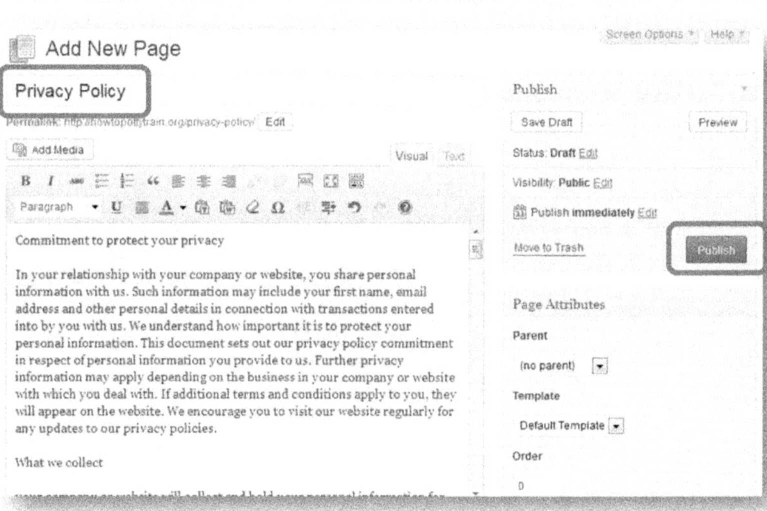

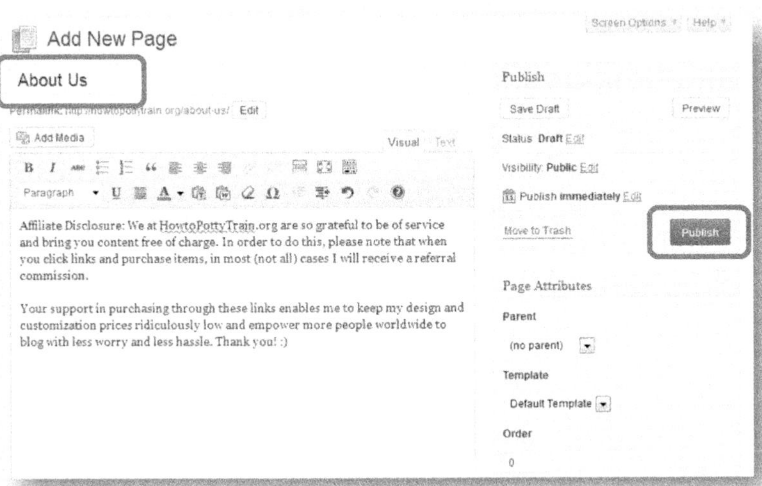

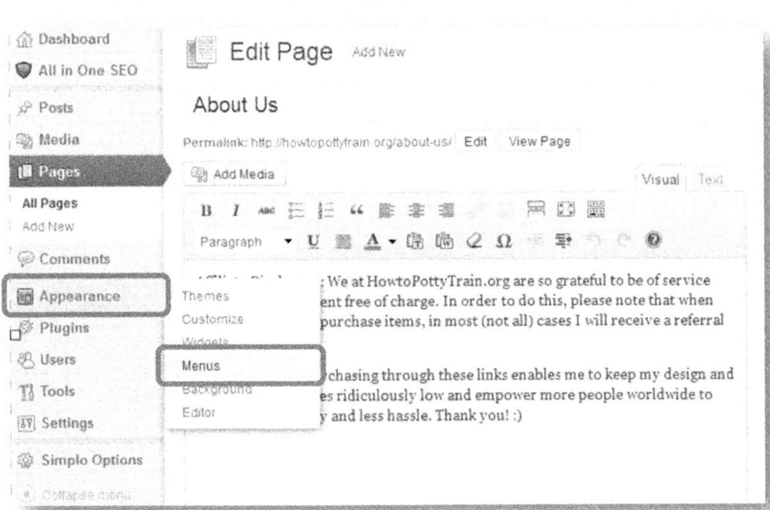

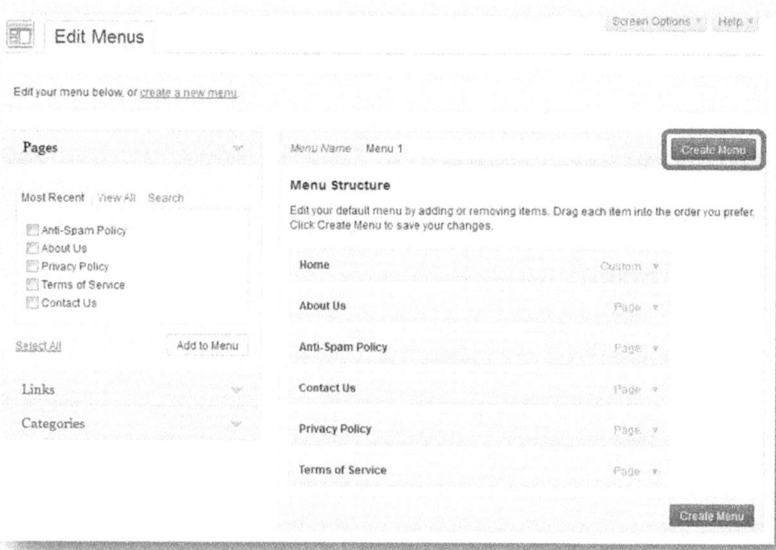

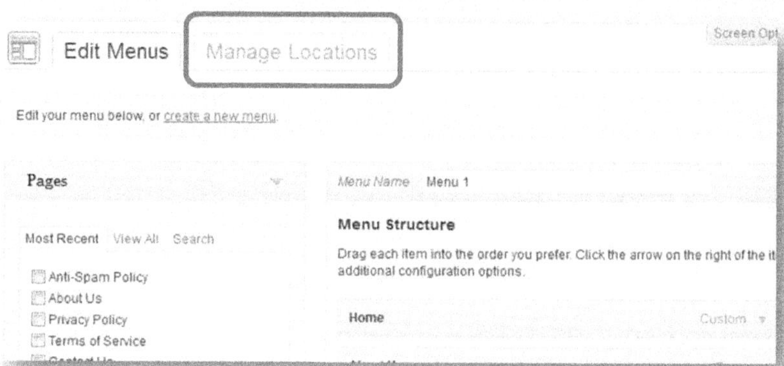

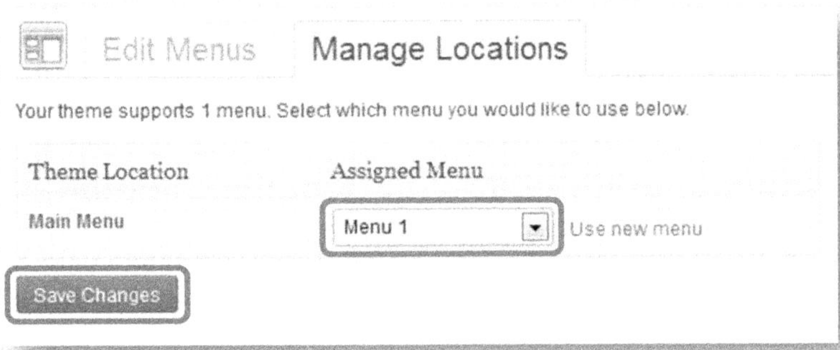

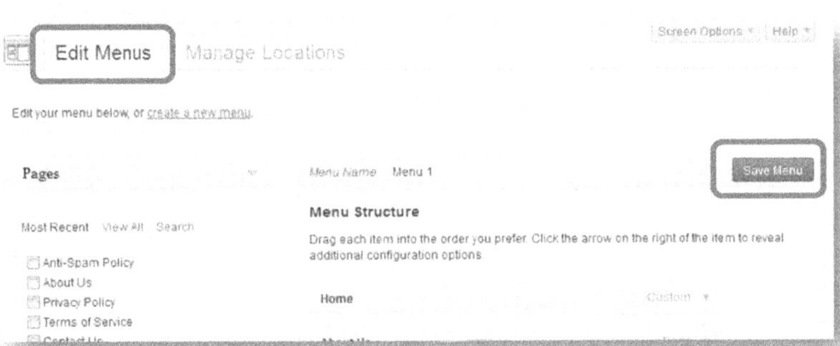

How to Potty Train your Kids

2. Social Buttons

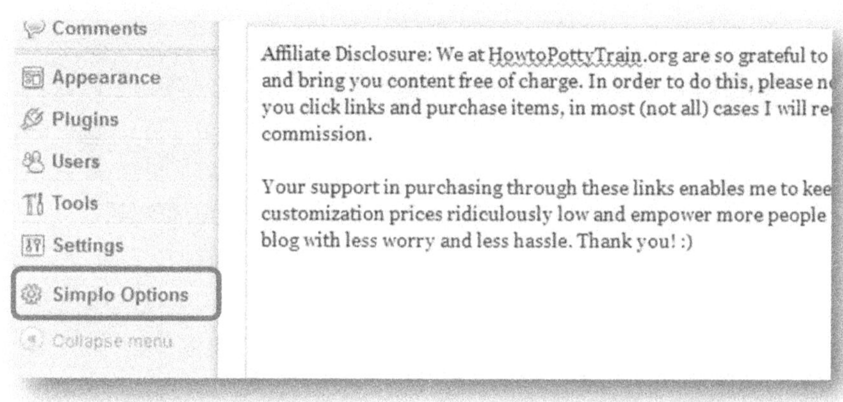

Remember to include your personal Social Link provided by every network.

3. Copyright information

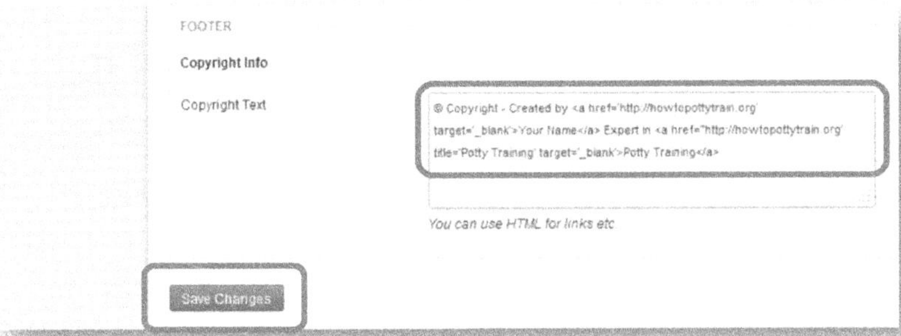

© Copyright - Created by <a href='http://howtopottytrain.org' target='_blank'>Your
Name</a> Expert in <a href="http://howtopottytrain.org' title='Potty Training'
target='_blank'>Potty Training</a>

4. Google Analytics

Now that the site is 100% ready, it is time to track all the visitors we will get to it with the most powerful traffic analysis service ever, Google Analytics. In order to get an account you need to have a Gmail account, which is free.

If you created brand new Gmail and Google Analytics accounts for your website (which I did) you will see something like this once you enter into your Google Analytics' account for the first time.

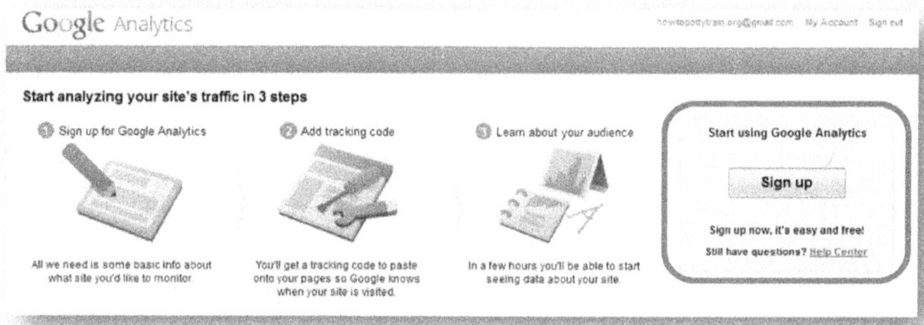

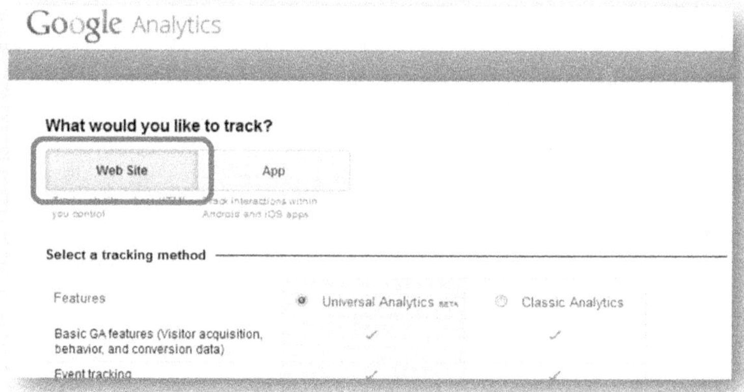

Setting up your web property

Website Name

Potty Training

Web Site URL

http:// ▼ howtopottytrain.org

Example: http://www.mywebsite.com

Industry Category new ⑦

We've added more Industry Categories! Select one that best represents your business

Healthcare ▼

Reporting Time Zone

United States ▼   (GMT-08:00) Pacific Time ▼

Setting up your account

Account Name

Accounts are the top-most level of organization and contain one or more tracking IDs

Potty Training

Data Sharing Settings ⑦

Data that is collected, processed, and stored in your Google Analytics account ("Google Analytics data") is secure and kept confidential. Google Analytics data is used to provide and improve service, to perform system critical operations, and in rare exceptions for legal reasons as described in our privacy policy.

The data sharing options give you more control over sharing your Google Analytics data. Learn more.

☐ **With other Google products only** optional

Enable enhanced ad features and an improved experience with AdWords, AdSense and other Google products by sharing your website's Google Analytics data with other Google services. Only Google services (no third parties) will be able to access your data. Show example

☐ **Anonymously with Google and others** optional

Enable benchmarking by sharing your website data in an anonymous form. Google will remove all identifiable information about your website, combine the data with hundreds of other anonymous sites in comparable industries and report aggregate trends in the benchmarking service. Show example

☐ **Account specialists** optional

Give Google marketing specialists and my Google sales specialists access to my Google Analytics data and account so they can find ways to improve my implementation and analysis, and share optimization tips with me. If I don't have dedicated sales specialists, give this access to authorized Google representatives

Learn how Google Analytics safeguards your data

[Get Tracking ID]   Cancel

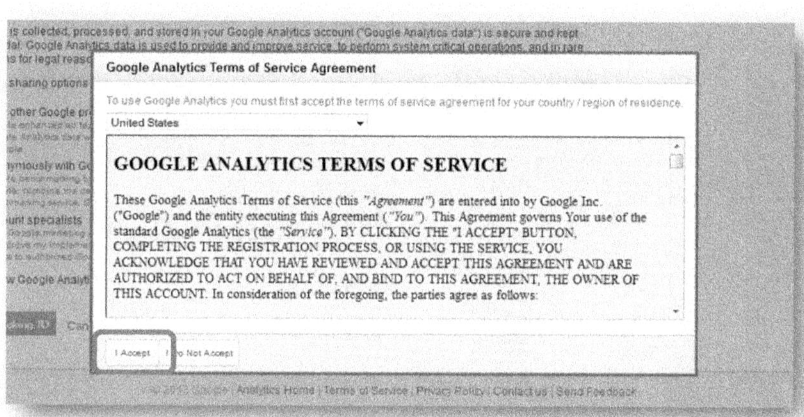

Google Analytics Terms of Service Agreement

To use Google Analytics you must first accept the terms of service agreement for your country / region of residence.

United States

GOOGLE ANALYTICS TERMS OF SERVICE

These Google Analytics Terms of Service (this "Agreement") are entered into by Google Inc. ("Google") and the entity executing this Agreement ("You"). This Agreement governs Your use of the standard Google Analytics (the "Service"). BY CLICKING THE "I ACCEPT" BUTTON, COMPLETING THE REGISTRATION PROCESS, OR USING THE SERVICE, YOU ACKNOWLEDGE THAT YOU HAVE REVIEWED AND ACCEPT THIS AGREEMENT AND ARE AUTHORIZED TO ACT ON BEHALF OF, AND BIND TO THIS AGREEMENT, THE OWNER OF THIS ACCOUNT. In consideration of the foregoing, the parties agree as follows:

I Accept   I Do Not Accept

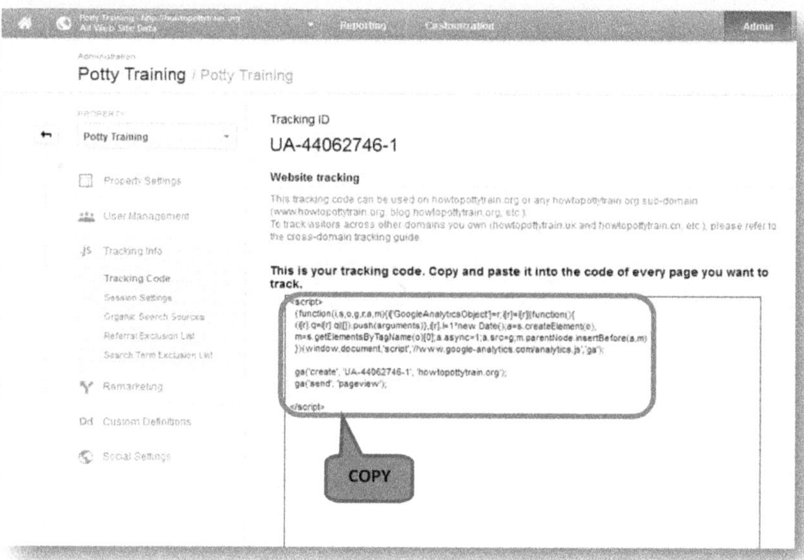

Administration
Potty Training / Potty Training

PROPERTY
Potty Training

Property Settings
User Management

JS   Tracking Info
Tracking Code
Session Settings
Organic Search Sources
Referral Exclusion List
Search Term Exclusion List

Remarketing

Dd   Custom Definitions

Social Settings

Tracking ID
UA-44062746-1

Website tracking

This tracking code can be used on howtopottytrain.org or any howtopottytrain.org sub-domain (www.howtopottytrain.org, blog.howtopottytrain.org, etc.).
To track visitors across other domains you own (howtopottytrain.uk and howtopottytrain.cn, etc.) please refer to the cross-domain tracking guide

This is your tracking code. Copy and paste it into the code of every page you want to track.

<script>
(function(i,s,o,g,r,a,m){i['GoogleAnalyticsObject']=r;i[r]=i[r]||function(){
(i[r].q=i[r].q||[]).push(arguments)},i[r].l=1*new Date();a=s.createElement(o),
m=s.getElementsByTagName(o)[0];a.async=1;a.src=g;m.parentNode.insertBefore(a,m)
})(window,document,'script','//www.google-analytics.com/analytics.js','ga');

ga('create', 'UA-44062746-1', 'howtopottytrain.org');
ga('send', 'pageview');

</script>

COPY

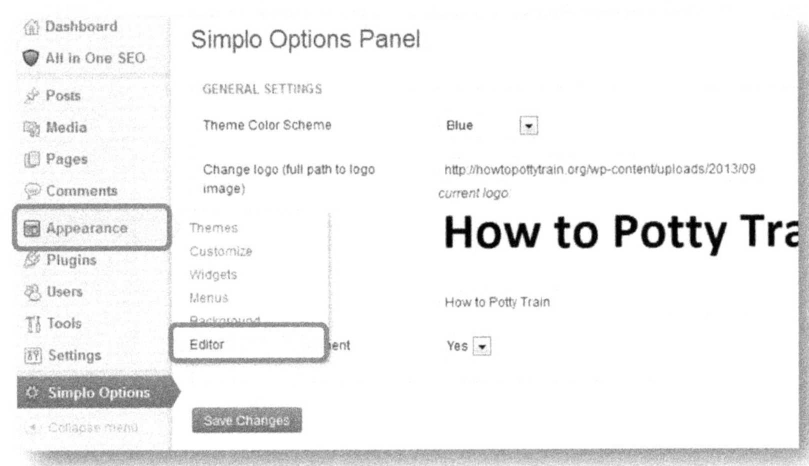

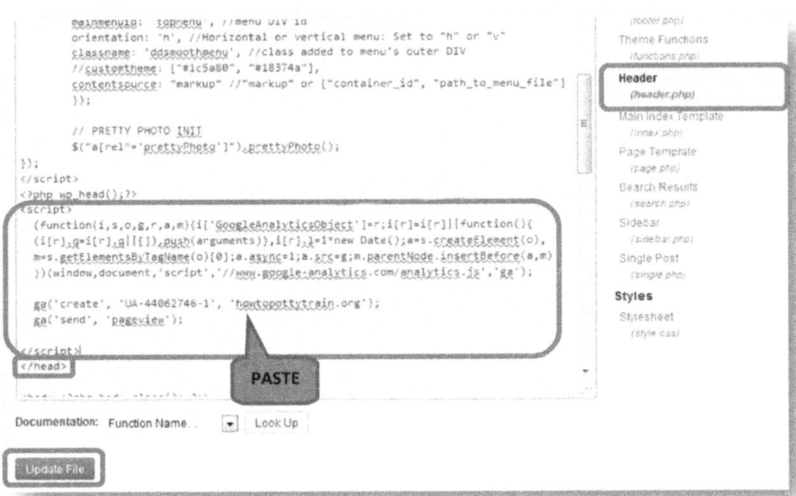

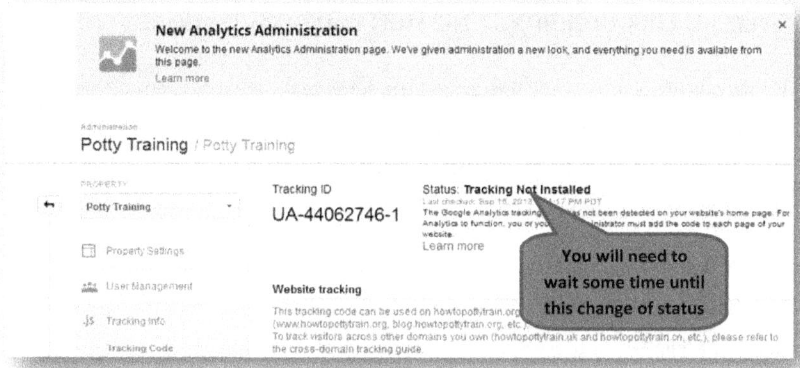

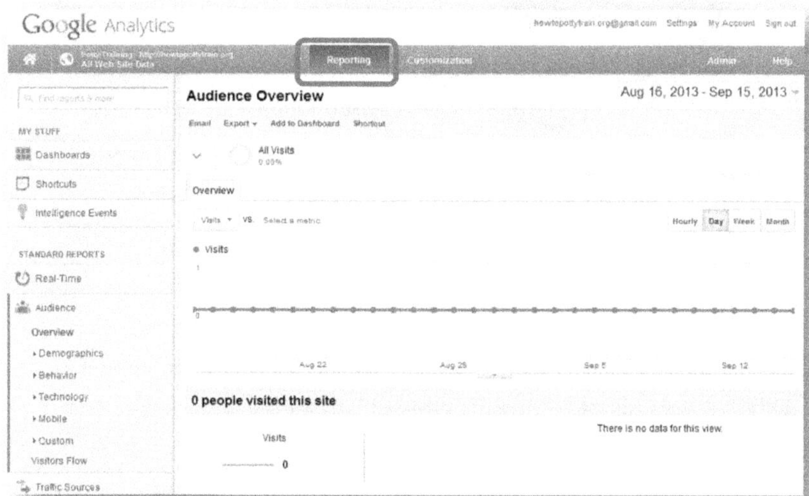

Now you are done with Step 9, and your site is 100% ready to start building some powerful backlinks safely and naturally.

Step 10: Link Building... the stuff that really works...

Finally our site is 100% ready to start getting some really great backlinks. This is probably the most important thing to rank your sites at the top. This is the evidence your site is important to other people and Google sees that, in order to recognize your website is of high quality.

Google does not accept automatic link building, specially boosting a website with backlinks from one day to another. That's why today it is harder to get high quality backlinks, but there is always a way to get them quick.

You don't need a great deal of backlinks anymore to rank your pages, Google cares on natural-authority-high quality backlinks. If you create the necessary amount of these kinds of backlinks to outrank your competitors that will be just enough to start out.

In this chapter you will see something you probably have not seen before, maybe you are waiting to see a list of techniques to build backlinks, but let me tell you I'm not going to waste your time on that. I will show you the stuff that really works.

There is not a greater way to show you what backlinks you should build than by spying on your own competitors. That is the only way you will know what backlinks Google cares about the most in order to rank that page at the top.

Remember Google is a coded robot, if you do the same and better than your competitors the bot will take you and place you on top of them.

What you are going to see is something that will really show you exactly what you sould be doing to your sites, and there you will discover what to do in order to master what are the backlinks that have the most powerful influence to rank pages at the top of Google.

Lets recap some information you saw in Step 3.

Backlinks: for a backlink (or link) we mean a hyperlink that is pointing to a specific place of a website (a page or to the domain itself). Backlinks may be internal or external. Internal backlinks are all those links pointing to different parts inside of the domain itself, like a link located in the home page liking to another one of its pages.

External Backlinks are the links that point at (target) any domain other than the domain the link exists on (source).

If another website links to you, this is considered an external link to your site. Similarly, if you link out to another website, this is also considered an external link.

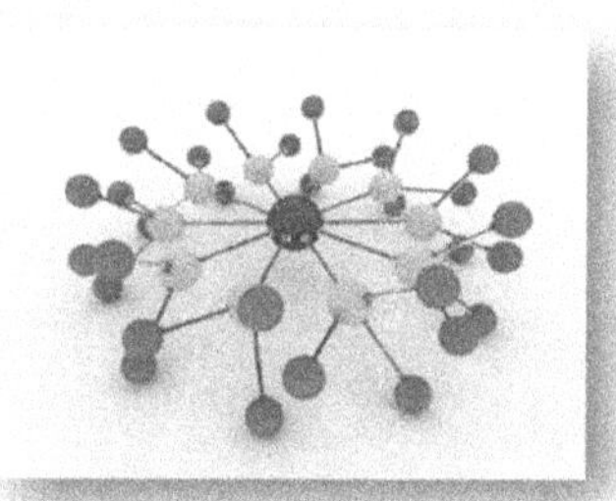

Experienced SEOs believe that external links are the most important source of ranking power. This is because external links pass "link juice" (ranking power) differently than internal links because the search engines consider them as third-party votes. (Taken from Moz.com)

What we will be looking for here is to spy on those competitors using again the greatest competition analysis software ever, the "Open Site Explorer" by Moz.com

Let's take "3 day potty training" as our sample audience to spy on our top competitors in Google in order to find a lot of great quality backlinks to build to our own pages.

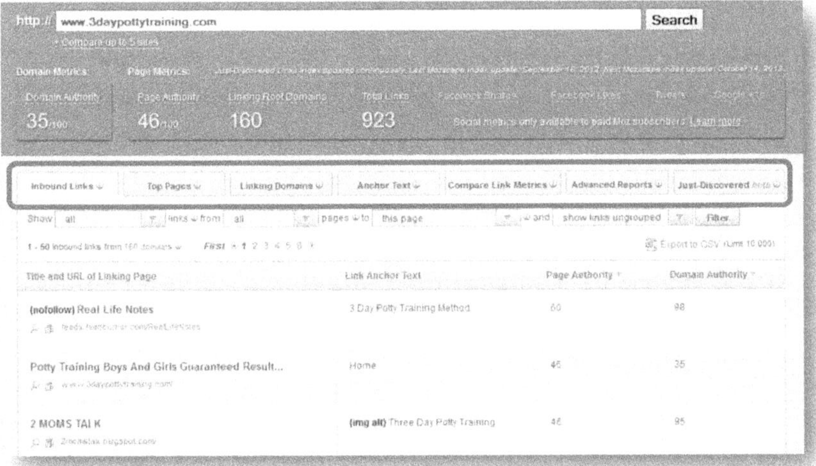

Here you see a whole great arsenal of competition analysis weapons that you can use to uncover every single competitor of your choice. The most important one is the inbound links feature.

With that one you are able to see great things like: follow or no-follow links, external or internal links and links to the page, domain or subdomain. You have everything you need to know in this great tool.

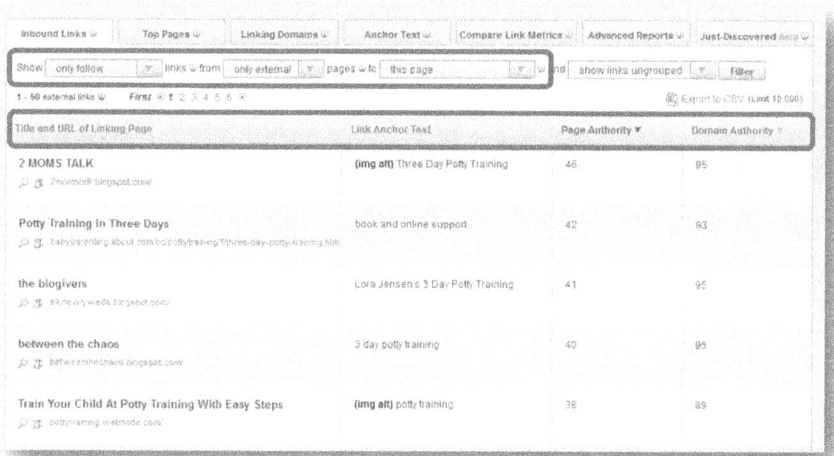

After you are done filtering the results of your choice you will able to see the Title, URL, anchor text and even the Page Authority and Domain Authority of the webpage where the backlinks were placed, this is just amazing.

Right there you can spy on the type of backlinks this competitor has built to his website so you can do the same, you can find out if the Backlinks is from a .edu or .gov sites, or if the backlinks are on a blog-roll from another authority site.

You can even find out if blog commenting and forum commenting backlinks still work or not. You can find out about any type of backlinks and stop wasting your time and being so worried about what type of backlinks to build.

You can do anything with this information, even up to the point of building your backlinks in the exact same spot that your competitor did. You can just follow his footsteps; this will save you a great deal of time on finding high quality backlinks.

Let's check on a weaker competitor to beat out of the top page of Google.

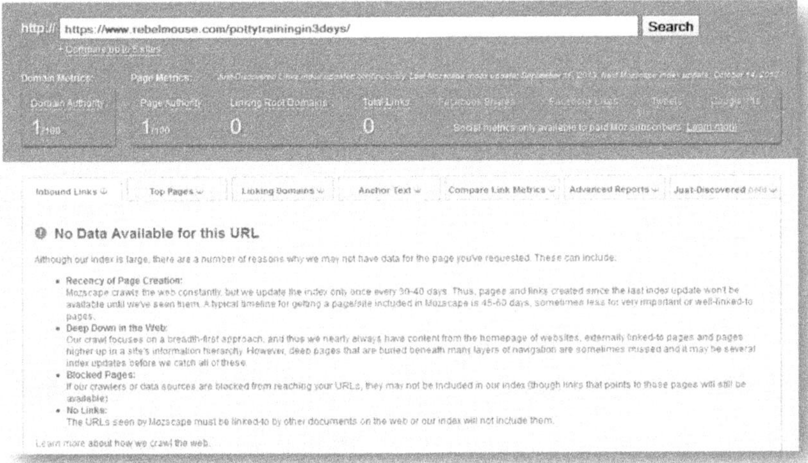

Well I guess there is not a weaker site than this. This is just a great chance for you to take its position by doing a way better job.

If you want to be able to find as much backlinks information as possible for your competitors, but you have reach your daily use of OpenSiteExplorer.org or you just can't afford the Moz.com monthly payment, you can always check Keyword Funnel Software, where you will be able to scrape up to 1,000 backlinks for every single url you submit into the scraper, all that data is legally scraped as well from the Moz.com golden databases.

You can get access to your free copy of Keyword Funnel Software by clicking here.

Conclusion:

SEO is extremely easy to manage. It happens the same way as with every single thing in life: things are not difficult. You just need to know where everything is and how you can properly use it – and that does it.

It is the same with SEO. Now that you know everything that you really need to position your business over the search engine results in the shortest time possible, you just need to apply it and do it for yourself.

Thanks so much for the time you have dedicated to learning how to get the most advantage out of the search engines for you and your business. Search Engines have come to stay in the market forever.

Millions and millions of dollars are often invested in search engines, and all of it is for both of us. Let's use it and reach our most precious business goals.

Resources

- **Google SEO Updates**
  - ✓ http://moz.com/google-algorithm-change

- **SEO Training**
  - ✓ https://support.google.com/webmasters/answer/35291?hl=en
  - ✓ https://www.google.com/webmasters/docs/search-engine-optimization-starter-guide.pdf
  - ✓ http://moz.com/beginners-guide-to-seo
  - ✓ http://searchengineland.com/guide/what-is-seo
  - ✓ http://www.seobook.com/
  - ✓ http://searchenginewatch.com/seo
  - ✓ http://blog.kissmetrics.com/simple-guide-to-seo/